Video Poker— Optimum Play

Dan Paymar

Publications by Dan Paymar:

Video Poker—Optimum Play

Video Poker Times™ (newsletter)

The Best of Video Poker Times™ (Volumes I and II)

Video Poker Anomalies & Anecdotes

Video Poker Cue Cards

ConJelCo titles:

Books

Winning Low-Limit Hold'em
by Lee Jones

Las Vegas Blackjack Diary
by Stuart Perry

Video Poker—Optimum Play
by Dan Paymar

Hold'em Excellence
by Lou Krieger

More Hold'em Excellence
by Lou Krieger

Software

Blackjack Trainer for the Macintosh or Windows

Ken Elliott's CrapSim for DOS

Percentage Hold'em for DOS

Stud & Hold'em Poker for Windows

Statistical Blackjack Analyzer for Windows

StatKing for Windows

Video Poker— Optimum Play

Dan Paymar

ConJelCo
Pittsburgh, Pennsylvania

Publisher's Cataloging-in-Publication Data

Paymar, Dan

Video Poker—Optimum Play/Dan Paymar.
   xii, 199 p. : ill. ; 22 cm.
ISBN 1-886070-11-3
I. Title.
Library of Congress Catalog Card Number: 98-73292

Revised Edition

1 3 5 7 9 8 6 4 2

Cover design by Lisa M. Lane
Cover photo courtesy of Casino Data Systems.

Precision Play™ and Video Poker Times™ are trademarks of Dan Paymar.

ConJelCo LLC
132 Radcliff Drive
Pittsburgh, PA 15237
[412] 492-9210
http://www.conjelco.com

Table of Contents

I first got acquainted with Dan Paymar over the Internet (we have only met electronically so far, but I hope to see him on my next trip to Las Vegas). I have been impressed with his openness and integrity in dealing with everyone who wants to learn about video poker. He has an excellent reputation in the world of video poker, and this new book is certain to increase his esteem. So, I was delighted when Chuck Weinstock asked me to write a foreword.

Dan Paymar has been one of the pre-eminent figures in the video poker world since the publication of his earlier book *Video Poker-Precision Play* in 1992. This new book will be a welcome addition to any video poker library. While the book is aimed primarily at novice to intermediate players, even seasoned veterans will be likely to learn something new.

Many people have heard that video poker can give the player an edge over the house. They may even know that some machines are "full pay," while others just can't be beaten. But, they don't take the time and trouble to learn what it takes to master the game. While there is no effortless way to learn, this book provides one of the quickest and easiest ways I know to move to the profitable side of video poker play.

Dan covers a lot more than just how to play video poker well. He gives clear and understandable explanations of how video poker machines work and why they can be beaten (and why good machines continue to exist, even though they can be beaten). Even a beginning player can use this book to quickly learn enough to pick good machines and play them well enough to win, or at least not lose too much. With a bit more effort, any reasonably intelligent student should be able to bring their mastery of the game up to a level that will turn the tables on the casinos.

Unlike some other books, this one is not just a compendium of strategies for a bewildering array of game variations. Instead, Dan focuses on three games (Jacks or Better, Deuces Wild and Joker Wild) and explains clearly how to play them well. He also gives enough information so that with just the aid of a hand calculator, you can figure out what many of the variations of these basic games are worth, and decide whether or not you should play them.

For those with a bit of mathematical skill and interest, Dan gives an excellent explanation of various techincal aspects of video poker (how strategy decisions are made, how to figure what to expect in the ups and downs of the game, bankroll requirment calculations, etc.). However, if you find math boring or intimidating, these sections can be skipped without reducing the overall value of the book. On the other hand, if you want to get serious about video poker, the tools are provided for you to go as far as you wish.

In some sections of the country (notably Atlantic City, where I play), video poker offerings are often not good enough to interest the serious player—unless you consider the bonuses and cash back the casinos offer to sweeten the pot. Dan has an excellent chapter on slot clubs and promotions that is a must for any player that wants to maximize their return for the time and risk the put into video poker. No one that plays more than casually should do without this information.

I wish I had this book when I began my video poker career—it would have saved me a lot of time and trouble (not to mention dollars!) If you study the contents carefully and put in the effort it takes to play well, this book will put you well on the way to becoming a video poker expert.

Jazbo
jazbo@jazbo.com
http://www.jazbo.com
July, 1998

Disclaimer

This book is not intended to encourage or approve of gambling except as a form of amusement. All calculations are based on the premise that the cards dealt by a video game are selected completely at random, such that each unseen card in the simulated deck always has an equal probability of appearing. Although that is mandated by Nevada gaming regulations, and we have no evidence to the contrary, no claim to that effect is intended.

Based on that premise, it is possible to be a long-term winner on certain machines. Note, however, that no amount of money or playing time can guarantee a jackpot, just as no system other than owning the house advantage, averaged over many games and many players, can guarantee a win in any gambling situation.

No warranty is made as to the suitability, usability or appropriateness of this product for any purpose. Neither the author, the publisher nor anyone involved in the development, publication or sale of this book shall be liable for any loss of time, money, anticipated revenues, or damages resulting from the use of this book or the strategies herein, even if they have been notified of the possibility of such loss. The full and total responsibility shall not exceed the original purchase price of this book.

Credits

The author wishes to thank the following people:

Chris Myers for his assistance in writing the original computer programs that were used to analyze the games and develop the hand-rank tables and Precision Play rules for this book.

Doug Reul, former associate editor of *Video Poker Times*, for his Volatility Index and other articles, for his assistance in polishing the strategies for some of the games, and for proof reading the manuscript for this book.

Bob Dancer for the 2nd Chance Progressive Strategy and other contributions to *Video Poker Times* and for some refinements to the strategies that have been adapted for this book.

Jeffrey Compton for *Video Poker Times* columns that were adapted for this book.

Norm Pos for *Video Poker Times* guest articles and his column on tournament play.

Jazbo Burns for precisely determining the expected payback of the Precision Play rules for Jacks-or-Better video poker.

Lenny Frome for getting me absorbed with being a long-term winner at video poker, for spurring my interest in analyzing the games, and for introducing me to the Poisson Distribution.

Video Poker Tutor, the analysis program from Panamint Software, which was used for some of the more recent refinements to the strategies.

Card Player magazine for a couple of quotations and for their support and cooperation.

The many readers of my earlier publications whose comments and questions led to improvements in this book.

Dedication

This book is dedicated to my wife, Mary, who has supported my commitment to video poker, who frequently joins me in playing the games (and eating the comped meals), and who has not complained about the bankroll fluctuations that occur in spite of always playing at an advantage.

This book is also dedicated to the memory of Lenny Frome, whose many publications, and his endeavor to have video poker declared "America's National Game of Chance," contributed more than any other writer to making video poker one of the most popular games in the casino. We learned of Lenny's death just shortly before going to press. We'll miss you, Lenny.

C ongratulations! By choosing this book, you are on your way to becoming a winner at video poker. Everyone who plays this exciting game will experience occasional wins, but most people wind up losers in the long run. If you put the information in this book to use, you will soon become a Precision player and a long term winner.

Did I hear you say that other books make this promise? True, the strategies in some of them do tell you the best plays and how to put them to use. But are you ready to memorize a 40- to 60-entry table or a very complex set of rules just to be able to play a game? And can you flawlessly recall such a strategy so you always make the best play? Unless your intention is to be a professional, you don't have to memorize detailed charts and perfect strategy. And even if you do intend to become a pro, this is an excellent place to start.

With Precision Play your decisions will be more accurate than they would be by following the "guidelines" or "tips" given in many books; yet Precision Play is easier to follow than most of the more general (and sometimes faulty) advice in many publications. But more importantly, Precision Play is designed for *optimum play* — that is, to generate the maximum expected hourly win rate. (This concept will be discussed more thoroughly in the sections "What Does 'Optimum Play' Really Mean?" on page 29 and "What Is Precision Play?" on page 33.)

By and large, this work is comprised of short article-like chapters, and while each one leads to the next, the purpose of using this style was to make each section readable and usable on its own. Though one chapter is sufficient for the basic theory and practice, subsequent sections offer more detail and additional hints.

This book will prepare you to get the most for your gaming dollar. Learn Precision Play, practice until you feel comfortable with it, and use the other sections of this book to make effective use of your bankroll.

No Cryptic Abbreviations. This book would be incomplete without expectancy (hand rank) tables for each playable starting hand. These are the mainstay of video poker as they give quick visual feedback and provide a consistent basis for a quick understanding of the potential for each video poker machine. But you won't see unnecessary and confusing abbreviations in these charts. The shortcuts I use are very intuitive and easy to read. More importantly, you do not have to memorize these tables. In fact, for the most common games, *you don't even have to look at the tables!* Instead, the strategies are reduced to a few simple rules that are easy to remember. You can use them without sacrificing any of your expected win rate.

Short-Pay Games Are Avoided. Some books are loaded with tables and charts for nearly every variety of video poker known even though most of those games are unattractive to a player whose objective is to be a winner. If short-pay games are the only ones you have access to and you insist on playing them, naturally, we recommend that you understand the correct strategies to help extend your bankroll. But, since the purpose of this book to make you a long term winner, any discussion of short-pay games — ones that do not offer a positive payback — is limited to recognizing and avoiding them.

No Prior Experience? If you have no experience with video poker then you must not skip the next three chapters. They are the backbone of this book. Appendix A on page 151 will acquaint you with the hands that are described in the games' payoff tables. Also, the practice sessions and the chapter "Practicing Video Poker At Home" on page 103 will help you get started *before your trip to the casinos.*

At the time this book was published, at least two Las Vegas area casinos had full-pay nickel Jacks-or-Better machines with a bonus royal flush jackpot, three had full-pay nickel Deuces Wild, and one had some nearly-full-pay nickel Joker Wild progressives (see Appendix C on page 172.) While you won't realize enormous profits from these machines, you can practice on them or just have fun on a small bankroll. As your play approaches the optimum, your expectancy will approach or exceed 100%, at which time, if your bankroll allows, you may want to step up to the 25¢ denominations.

A Guaranteed Win? Well, almost; but there are two things to consider. First, the calculations and discussions in this book are based on the presumption that each machine uses an independent, unbiased random number generator which "shuffles" the deck before each hand so each card has an equal probability of appearing at any time. Thus, the games very closely approximate the laws of probability so that the payback is determined almost entirely by the payoff schedule and your decisions.

Second, *long term payback must be stressed.* In the short run, your actual cash flow is likely to fluctuate widely, both above and below the projected win rate. You could hit a jackpot on your first roll of quarters, or you might go through a large bankroll without ever hitting one (see "Probability of a Jackpot (or of No Jackpot)" on page 119). There are no guarantees except that following the advice in this book will give you the best chance of becoming a long-term winner.

What Is The Long Term? Since the rated payback includes the royal flush jackpot, which on average occurs only once every 37,000 to 48,000 plays, I consider the long term to be at least 250,000 plays. This may sound like an unrealistic number for practical purposes, but as you become experienced you will probably be making in excess of 500 plays per hour. Therefore, the long term may be less than 500 hours of active play. If you are playing 30 or more hours per week, the long term could be as short as a few months.

Hate Mathematics? Don't worry. Although there are many calculations showing how the strategies and bankroll recommendations were derived, they are not crucial to your play. You may skip all of the mathematics without reducing the accuracy of your play or your chances of being a long term winner. The examples are included for the more mathematically inclined who may wish to extend the results to other situations or other variations of the three basic games and for those who just like to see verification in black and white.

Hungry for More? If you would like to keep up to date on the latest games, with information about where to find them and how to play them, you should read *Video Poker Times.* This bimonthly newsletter is invaluable for all players, whether recreational or professional. Even if you risk only a few hundred dollars a year on video poker, the information in each issue will more than pay for the cost of a subscription. (See Appendix E on page 180 for more information.)

Chapter 1

What Is Video Poker?

It may sound silly to define video poker at first. But, it's surprising how many people think and act as if the game is "just like poker." They use tactics (holding kickers, looking for a bluff, for example) that work at the table but are costly at the machine. It's extremely important that you understand the differences.

At one time, draw poker and five-card stud were very popular forms of live table poker, but they have been almost completely displaced by newer table games such as seven-card stud, Texas hold'em and Omaha. In home games the "simple" forms of poker have been embellished with a variety of wild cards to increase interest and excitement. Today, five-card draw poker is enjoying a resurgence in the form of video poker. Over the years, these games have seen some of the home-game "enhancements" thrown in to attract more players. Regardless of the similarities, video poker is unique in that it is one of very few games developed for casino use before being played privately.

Video poker resembles the traditional slot machine in several ways. The machine is housed in a similar metal cabinet with similar locks; it has a coin slot to accept your bet and a coin hopper that pays out your winnings; it makes various sounds to attract players. Many have a slot club card reader and/or a bill acceptor. Like many new reel slots, video poker games display the results on a screen instead of mechanical reels.

The most obvious difference is that on a reel slot the player wins when the symbols stop with a particular combination such as three bars, while a video poker player wins when the final five cards form a recognizable poker hand, such as a straight. The most important difference, however, is that the video poker player has an opportunity to select which cards to hold and then draw in an attempt to improve the hand. The player needs a certain degree of skill because the key to achieving the game's rated payback is making the most accurate selection.

In either case, all of the winning combinations with their respective payoffs are shown on the front of the machine or on the screen, and the machine automatically pays out the indicated number of coins (or counts up that number of credits) when one of those combinations occurs.

What most players don't know (or at least won't consciously admit to themselves) is that in nearly all modern gambling machines, the decision is made by an internal digital computer as soon as the first coin is deposited or any bet-button is pressed. The reels are then spun by independent motors to display that outcome. Unlike older machines, which were randomized mechanically with the result undetermined until the reels actually stopped, the new machines are controlled by a random number generator that is programmed into the internal computer. Obviously it would be possible to program such a machine to avoid or cut the frequency of certain payoffs. However, Nevada Gaming Control regulates and tests the machines to assure that they are random enough so the long-term payback is as it should be and the possible outcomes occur in the proper proportion. Thus, even though the mechanical operation of the reels has nothing to do with the result except to display it, the outcome of each individual play is still determined randomly (within the constraints of the machine's assigned probabilities).

Many casinos advertise high paybacks on reel slots. It's not uncommon to see claims that a casino has machines that pay 97% or better, but this often applies only to certain $1 machines. Care to guess what the payback is on the others? Without knowing the machine's internal logic, it's impossible to calculate. But if 97% payback is considered generous, then what do the others pay? Nevada gaming regulations specify only that a machine must pay back at least 75% of all money wagered (see Appendix D on page 176). In New Jersey the minimum is 83%. Many other jurisdictions do not specify a minimum payback. Worse, some new gambling areas specify a *maximum* payback (most likely to assure a flow of tax dollars).

I have seen 92% advertised as the world's highest payback on video keno. What do other keno machines pay? (Live keno pays back only 67% to 79%, so relatively speaking I suppose that 92% could be considered liberal.) Also, lower denomination machines of all types generally have a lower percentage payback so the casino can still make a profit on their investment and the floor space.

Just what does 97% payback mean to you? To get a realistic feeling for that *generous* return, try this: Throw three dollars into a box, then reach in and take back $2.91 (97% of $3). Repeat this five hundred times, then throw the box (and the $45 it now contains) in the trash. Does this make sense? Yet this is equivalent to your expectancy after about one hour of moderately fast play on a 97% return, three-coin, dollar slot machine. Of course in the short term you might get lucky and be a big winner, but in the long run, you are paying an average of $45 per hour for the "fun" of feeding that machine.

Compare the very best reel machine's maximum of perhaps 99% payback to a *minimum* 99.5% payback when you use the easy *Precision Play* method with recommended video poker machines. And that's just the beginning. On many poker machines you really can achieve over 100% long-term payback. Even some nickel machines offer over 100% potential. Is it any wonder that video poker has become so popular? Yet most people don't know the difference between full pay and short pay. Worse yet, they don't bother learning how to play well or even how to recognize the good games. Some payback schedules are so bad that the maximum payback is 90% or less.

Video poker does have an element of luck, governed by a random number generator[1] programmed into its internal computer just as the reel slots. But unlike a reel slot (where you just pull the handle and hope for the best), video poker injects the element of skill, which often makes the payback attractive. After being dealt your initial five cards, you have the opportunity to hold some of the cards and draw to replace the others in an attempt to effect a winning poker hand (or to improve an existing winner) just as you would do in a live draw poker game. If the final hand is in the payoff schedule, the machine makes the payoff, either by counting up credits or dropping coins; otherwise, your bet is lost.

---

[1]Since it is impossible to generate truly random numbers algorithmically, it is more technically correct to call it a "pseudo-random number" generator. However, it is random enough that the machine lives up to the expectations presented in the payoff schedule. Some players have reported anomalies in certain games, but the discussion of such aberrations (if they even exist) is beyond the scope of this book. If these things interest you, see Appendix E on page 180 for my new booklet, *Video Poker Anomalies & Anecdotes*.

The main attractions of video poker are that the player's wits are pitted against the machine, the action is fast, and besides appearing to be a good gamble, players have a chance at a big jackpot. To the skilled player, however, the attraction is that some games offer an opportunity for a long-term profit. Just as in a live poker game, there is a considerable amount of risk and luck involved in the short term, but it is a player's skill that will make the difference between a winner and a loser in the long run.

You may have bought this book because you already knew that some video poker games offer over 100% potential long-term payback. The key word, though, is "potential." Some players seem to think they will get that payback regardless of how they play. Realistically, you will achieve a game's rated payback *only* if you always hold the cards that will give the highest expected value (the average payback for all possible outcomes) for each hand you are dealt. That is why I call video poker "The Intelligent Player's Slot Machine."

The first step in winning takes place before you even start to play. Only a small percentage of the wide variety of games can be beat in the long run, so you must first learn how to recognize those games. Primarily you are looking for a game that offers over 100% payback. Next, you must know how to play to achieve that payback. I frequently see people playing short-pay machines while the one next to it — the same basic type but full-pay — sits idle. Then, through simple errors in selecting discards, following hunches or "intuition," they may be giving up yet another five percent or more. In some cases, however, a slot club or special promotion adds enough so that an otherwise unattractive game becomes quite attractive; this is particularly true in Atlantic City, and it is becoming more true all the time in other areas.

Yet we must be grateful to those unskilled players. Without them, such opportunities could not exist; the casinos would always lose money on the good games and take them out.

> *"Let us be thankful for the fools. But for them, the rest of us could not succeed."*—Mark Twain

Now that we know that good opportunities really exist, we can get started. Having selected an attractive game, it is then your task to select which cards to hold to maximize your expected payoff for each hand dealt. Selecting a good game and consistently making the correct play will make you a winner in the long run. Making frequent wrong plays, whether intentionally due to hunches or simply because you haven't learned the correct play, will guarantee being a loser. It is this element of skill that has resulted in video poker becoming the fastest growing game in the casino. Sometimes the correct play is obvious, but quite often it is far from intuitive. The goal of this book is to teach you to become a winning player. More importantly, my goal is to make it as easy as possible for you to be a long term winner.

While it is true that games offering over 100% payback may be rare outside southern Nevada, following the strategies in this book will minimize your losses and give you the best chance of having a winning session.

Getting Started

If you are already quite familiar with video poker, or if you are in a hurry to get to the meat of this book, you may be tempted to skip this chapter, but it would be better to read it anyway. You may discover that you missed something before, and every little bit of knowledge can add to your enjoyment and winnings.

The mechanics of playing video poker are simple. Having selected a machine, you should insert your player's card. If the casino has a slot club and you don't have a card, you should get one before you begin playing. This is very important since the slot club rebate may make up a significant portion of your expected win rate. Better yet, get two cards in case you want to play two machines. Also, you will have a spare in case you forget and leave one in a machine or the magnetic strip gets damaged.

If you are not familiar with the game of poker, or if you encounter a game with hands you don't recognize, be sure to read Appendix A on page 151. And perhaps more importantly, if you are familiar with live table poker and think that video poker is just like it, then be sure to read the section on "Video Poker vs. Live Draw Poker" on page 8.

To begin a hand, insert the number of coins you want to play. Although most machines accept from one to five coins, some accept only three or four, some accept eight or ten, and a few accept up to one hundred coins. The serious player always plays at least the number of coins required to qualify for the full per-coin payoff on all jackpots (five coins on most machines). On many games you get paid only 250-for-1 for a royal flush with fewer coins played instead of 800-for-1 when you play five coins. Under some circumstances, however, it may be better for a recreational player with a very limited bankroll to play just one coin (but read "One Coin vs. Five Coin Play" on page 115 before you do this).

Most machines automatically deal if the maximum number of coins has been inserted. To play for fewer coins you must press the Deal button after inserting the coins. However, some machines offer a "replay" option, usually by pressing the Deal/Draw button, which automatically bets the same number of credits as the preceding play and starts the deal.

After you insert the maximum number of coins or press the Max Bet, Deal/Draw or Replay button, the machine "deals" your first five cards. Most machines let you know if you have a made payoff immediately by beeping and displaying the hand type. A few even highlight or select the cards that make up that pay for you, but it is always your choice as to which cards to keep. As you might have guessed, it is sometimes correct to break up a made pay; for example, you would break a dealt straight in favor of a four-card royal flush.

You select which cards you want to keep by pressing the corresponding Hold buttons. On most machines, you press the same Hold (or Hold/Cancel) button to deselect a card, but a few (mostly older) machines require pressing a separate Clear button and then starting the selection process over again. Some of the newest machines have touch-sensitive screens, allowing you to select which cards to hold simply by touching their image on the screen. You can also touch the screen for the Bet and Deal functions, but most serious players use the buttons in preference to the touch screen for all functions because it's much faster. In any case, the word "hold" or "held" appears on the screen above, below or across the center of each card as it is selected.[2]

When you are satisfied with your selection, press the Draw (or Deal/Draw) button. Typical machines then display card backs in place of the cards not held, before showing the new cards in their place. That's it then. The game is over. If you have a winning hand, the machine automatically counts up credits or pays out coins according to the payoff schedule.

Most modern machines are set up for credit play. That is, your wins count up credits instead of automatically dropping coins, thus letting you make your next bet from those credits instead of inserting coins. Some even offer your choice of playing credits or inserting coins for each play by having a Cash/Credit button (instead of the usual Pay Out button). For credit play on the latter type of machine, you would press this button so it is lit.

Assuming you are playing at over 100% expected payback, your expected win rate is in direct proportion to your playing speed, so you should always use credit play for maximum speed. Press the Max Bet button to play the maximum number of coins, or press the Replay or Deal button to play the same number of coins as for the preceding play if the machines has such a feature. In either case, this starts the deal. Alternatively, if you want to bet fewer than maximum coins, press the Bet button once for each credit to be bet followed by the Deal button to deal the cards.

When you decide to quit playing, press the Collect (or Pay Out or Cash/Credit) button, and the machine will pay out a number of coins equal to your credits. If you have a very large number of credits, part or all of it may be hand paid by a slot attendant.[3] Also, the machine's hopper may be emptied during the payout, requiring a slot attendant for a hopper fill. Don't leave the machine with credits still showing.

---

[2]Some brands of machines are just the opposite — you select the cards to be *discarded* instead of those to hold, and those cards immediately disappear from the screen. If you think you may have made a mistake, you have to select your discards again to see what they were. This can make for very slow play. Until recently you would encounter these unintuitive machines in southern Nevada only in bars and restaurants rather than in a casino, but the VLC "coin free" machines which operate like this are becoming more popular. Such machines, however, very rarely offer an attractive game, so you probably won't be playing them anyway.

[3]A few casinos have tested "coinless" machines, which are also available in some Indian casinos. There is no coin slot, and they accept only currency or coupons. When you "cash out" a coupon is printed which may be taken to the cashier and exchanged for cash or inserted into another machine instead of cash. Unfortunately, the machines have not been very popular with players. Maybe we're not ready for a coinless casino. The noise of dropping coins seems to be a big part of the attraction of a casino to most people.

Many machines now have bill acceptors that allow you to insert a $1, $5, $10 or $20 bill which is converted to the appropriate number of credits according to the denomination of the machine. Some machines also accept $50 and $100 bills. The bill acceptors can be finicky; if they don't accept your bill, try turning it around, smoothing it flat, or holding on lightly as it is being drawn in.

Most machines also have a button labeled "Change" or "Service." Pressing this button turns on a light on top of the machine, indicating that you want assistance. (Don't use this light for cocktails; you will just unnecessarily bother the people who bring change, get hopper fills, pay off jackpots, and so forth. The cocktail servers come around at regular intervals, but they don't look for these lights.)

Playing video poker is that easy. To become a winning player, however, requires that you not only select a game that offers over 100% return but also that you learn the correct strategy for that particular game. To get started in winning at video poker, I recommend that you select only one basic game and learn to play it accurately. I suggest Deuces Wild if full-pay machines are available where you play since it is the most common game that offers significantly more than 100% payback. Otherwise, I recommend Jacks-or-Better.

Video Poker vs. Live Draw Poker

Other than the fact that it's played on a machine, video poker appears at first glance to be nearly identical to a live draw poker game — you are dealt five cards, you choose which ones to hold, you draw to replace your discards in an attempt to improve your hand.

As a result of this similarity, a poker player who is not entirely familiar with video poker could be prone to making certain errors. Although the basic hand types are the same, video poker is not poker. Here are some of the critical differences:

- In order to win more money in a live poker game, you must bet more during the hand. In most video poker games you are not allowed to increase your bet, nor are you ever put at risk for more than your initial bet, yet it's possible to win many times your bet if you end up with a good hand.

- In live poker you can bluff in an attempt to convince another players that you have a strong hand. By betting when other players appear to be weak, it is sometimes possible to win a pot even though you don't have the best hand. In video poker you can never bluff, nor can you win with any final hand less than the lowest hand on the payoff schedule.

• Instead of trying to make a better hand than your live-game opponents in order to win a pot, your only goal is trying to make a hand that will generate a payoff. Such things as a kicker, the ranks of two pair, or how high the top end of a flush or a straight is, have no significance in most video poker games.

• In live draw poker, holding a "kicker" (an unmatched card, usually an ace) with a pair may sometimes be a good play. Besides the possibility of making two pair, aces up, this gives you deceptive value; that is, your opponents may think you're drawing to three of a kind. Since deception is of absolutely no value in video poker, and two pair pays the same regardless of the ranks, holding a kicker only reduces the chances of making three of a kind or better.

The most common error player make in any video poker game is holding too many cards. More than any other version of the game, Deuces Wild offers even more opportunities to make errors through hunches or false concepts. One common error is to hold one or more high cards when there is nothing to go with them. A high pair is not a paying hand in Deuces Wild; high cards have the same value as low cards (other than deuces).

To play video poker correctly you must set aside many of the concepts of live poker. Live poker is a game of mathematics and people, with the people aspect growing in importance as the stakes increase. Video poker is strictly a game of solitary mathematics regardless of the denomination. (However, it may be correct to consider the effects of other players on your game if you are playing a machine that is tied into a bank with a very large common progressive payoff that will reset to a low value when anyone on the bank of machines hits it.)

A Brief History of Video Poker

Compared to games such as craps, blackjack and poker, video poker is a relatively new game. First introduced in a few Las Vegas casinos in 1978, the "video" game of Draw Poker obviously offered a challenge to the player's skill, and people got in line to test their wits against the machine. However, the manufacturer apparently hadn't yet figured out how to accurately determine the game's maximum payback, so the payoff schedule was very conservative (on the casino's side, naturally). You may still find some of these original machines around downtown Las Vegas, in some small casinos in other areas, and offered for sale in the slot machine stores. You will recognize them by one or more of the following characteristics:

1. The payoff for a high pair is not shown in the original payoff schedule. Instead, there is a placard stuck on the machine saying "BET RETURNED ON A PAIR OF JACKS OR BETTER."

2. Unless the buttons have been replaced, they are flush with the surface of the playing area and must be pressed in to make contact.

3. There are probably separate buttons for Deal and Draw.

4. Instead of pressing a Hold button a second time to cancel the hold, there may be a Clear or Cancel button that cancels all holds.

5. The graphics are not very good, and the word "HELD" may be a different color for each card.

6. It does not provide for credit play; instead, coins are immediately dropped for each payoff.

Nearly all modern machines have one Deal/Draw button and five Hold/Cancel buttons, and all buttons are raised for easier play. Most allow credit play, many also accept paper currency, and all have cleaner screen graphics.

The low payback of those original machines, resulting from the first payoff being on two pair (only a bit over 81% maximum, and probably around 75% for most players), quickly squelched the enthusiasm, and the game received very little extended play.

The casinos reacted to the waste of floor space by telling the manufacturer to do something to get more play or take the machines out. The manufacturer responded by modifying the program chip to pay one-for-one on a pair of jacks or higher, hence the placard mentioned above. Besides raising the payback to a level the players would accept, this accomplished what no other casino game had done — it turned a push (no exchange of money) into an apparent win (by returning the player's bet, which had already disappeared into the guts of the machine, and flashing "winner" on the screen). The result was the popular game we now refer to as Jacks-or-Better even though the machines may still say Draw Poker or Classic Poker on the glass panels.

They also added a progressive jackpot on some machines or on banks of machines. (These are "connected" by computers so the jackpot increases each time a player on any single machine inserts a coin.) Since the players' money now lasted longer, perhaps even longer than for the same level of play on a reel slot, the machines began to get a lot of action. Naturally, the casinos started allocating more floor space to them.

The surprising aspect was that a few players seemed to be making money playing video poker. Others wondered whether there was a better way to play—other than guessing or aping table poker tactics. If some players were beating the casinos at their own game because there was a better way to play, then how could the average player learn to play that way?

This question was partially answered in 1981 when David Sklansky's short article "Poker Machine Strategy" was published in *Casino and Sports* magazine. In the article, Sklansky, a noted gaming theorist and poker player, showed that the house edge was relatively small compared to other casino games, that money could be made at the game under certain circumstances, and that there really was a "best" way to play each dealt hand.

However, none of the early games offered more than 100% payback with the basic 4,000-coin royal flush, so the only possible way to make a profit was to play a progressive when the jackpot was high enough to push the total payback significantly over 100%. The problem was that no one was sure just where that point was because no one had yet worked out an accurate strategy. To learn how to get the most out of such an opportunity we had to wait until 1984 for an article in Volume 6 of *Stanford Wong's Blackjack Newsletters* for an accurate analysis and strategy.

Wong followed this in 1988 with *Professional Video Poker*, which is still in print (revised 1991, 1993). Wong offered his strategy based on break-even points and strategy modifications to take the best advantage of progressive jackpots. Although this may still be one of the best books available for Jacks-or-Better progressive enthusiasts, the strategy may be somewhat difficult for the average player to use in a casino.

Next came Lenny Frome's *Expert Video Poker for Las Vegas* in 1989. Frome's book was the first work to present practical video poker strategies that could be used in the casinos by a recreational player. It also was the first to show how to get an edge over the casino on a non-progressive game (Joker Wild, Kings or Better, paying 20-for-1 for four-of-a-kind).

Thanks to these early works, many players were attracted to the new game, and video poker became an overwhelming success. But perhaps more significantly, some serious gamblers (i.e., players who will rarely get involved with any game where they can't get an edge) started spending many hours on certain machines.

Many other writers have entered the fray with books, booklets and articles on video poker. These books range from useful to useless (or worse).

Some authors — genuine experts on poker, blackjack and other varieties of gambling — have included information on video poker in their books. Some promise to show you how to make a fortune by gambling. Unfortunately the video poker chapters are rarely of any value, either because they are incomplete or because the information they impart is only partially accurate. Often, the advice is based on erroneous or obsolete concepts. The reader has confidence in the writer because other parts of the book seem to be accurate and useful, but the video poker chapter misleads the reader and costs him money. (In general, you are always safer selecting a book that concentrates on one facet of gaming.)

Today there are many different versions of video poker. The original Draw Poker, with the first payoff starting at two pair, is (thankfully) extinct; but, its successor, Jacks-or-Better, remains fairly popular in spite of all the newer variations. It is included in this book because in many casinos its maximum payback of 99.5439% makes it the lowest house edge of any game offered. But, of course, we're looking for even better opportunities.

The first major variation on the basic Draw Poker game was Joker Wild, which was quite popular at first but was soon overshadowed by Deuces Wild. Although in their full pay versions both games offer over 100% payback, the correct strategies are anything but intuitive, so very few people ended up winners. Other variations soon followed.

With more manufacturers cropping up, new games now appear almost weekly, so it is impossible for one book to give the correct strategy for all of them. It would not be worth the effort anyway since the vast majority of the games are under 100% payback even with the best play. Of course there is the rare exception of a new game that is very attractive, and casinos often make errors in setting pay schedules or designing promotions. When this happens, the player has to be prepared to take advantage immediately because the attractive qualities might not last long. (These are but two of the compelling reasons to read *Video Poker Times*.)

Types of Video Poker Players

When discussing discrimination, musical satirist Tom Lehrer once said something to this effect: "Some people divide people into two categories — those we like and those we don't like — and I just *hate* people like that." That just about sums up how I feel about the way in which some people play video poker. Don't go on the defensive about the categories that follow. I will describe seven general types of video poker players, but there is considerable overlap, so you might find that you fit into more than one group. If you plan to become a Precision player, you should determine where you currently stand so you will have some idea of how much work is ahead of you.

The vast majority of players fall into the first two groups. These are the unfortunate losers who keep the casinos happy and create the good opportunities for the rest of us. Don't be alarmed or discouraged if you find that you fall into one of these groups; you will soon advance to type three or four, and perhaps eventually to type five. It is my sincere hope that you are not a type six or seven. It's up to you to decide where you fit in and where you want to go from there.

1. *The novice.* The typical novice is a purely recreational player who is attracted to the game by its speed (lots of action), apparent low cost[4] (as little as 5¢ per play), and the fact that in most games the top jackpot is won by the glorious royal flush (the highest hand in live poker). Unfortunately for them (but fortunate for the skilled players as well as the casino), these people makes numerous errors that cost them money and increase the

house edge by two to five percent. This translates into a two to five percent additional loss for the individual.

2. *The somewhat-advanced player.* These players probably spend a lot of time in the casinos. They have learned to play above novice level, either by reading a book or through experience alone. They have not learned an accurate strategy fully, so they could be giving up as much as two percent to the house. The somewhat-advanced player does well enough that video poker becomes low cost entertainment for him with a good prospect of an occasional win. The rare royal flush, or the more frequent small jackpots on some games, keep them coming back. They may value comps more than an edge on the game itself.

3. *The serious player.* He may be an infrequent visitor or a regular, but what sets the serious player apart is that he has made the effort to learn reasonably accurate play for at least one game, and he plays only the games where his skill can yield over 100% long-term payback (including comps or other side benefits). He may lack the bankroll necessary to ride out the large fluctuations on a high denomination game so he limits himself to the quarter machines (or perhaps even to nickels). Although he has an edge, his expected hourly win rate is generally less than six dollars per hour, but comps and promotions may more than double that. Video poker provides a long-term gain for this player, but it is probably as much a source of entertainment as of income.

4. *The semiprofessional.* This is a skilled player who supplements his income by playing video poker. He probably has a regular job or is retired, and he very likely plays for both enjoyment and gain. He may be playing quarters or dollars, or even higher stakes, depending on his bankroll and comfort level, but as long as he doesn't overplay his bankroll he will be a winner in the long run. He also gets a lot out of slot clubs, comps and special promotions.

---

[4]The seemingly low cost may be deceiving. Even a typical novice playing five nickels per hand at a very slow rate of four hands per minute is wagering $60 per hour and has an expected loss rate of about $2 to $5 per hour while waiting for a royal flush. Skilled players are generally much faster, playing 600 to 1,000 hands per hour. By playing two $1 machines simultaneously, a pro might be wagering as much as $7,500 per hour. But of course this isn't unique to video poker; the action may be even faster on a reel slot.

5. *The professional.* This is a highly skilled player who may depend upon video poker as his primary source of income. He has several attributes that most other players may lack, including the aptitude to learn a new game quickly, the ability to play several games at near-perfect accuracy for many hours a day, the discipline to always make the mathematically correct play, and a bankroll sufficient to ride out the fluctuations on the games. And perhaps more importantly, he knows how to evaluate promotions and extract the most from them as well as comps and regular slot club benefits. The pro treats video poker as a job, spending long hours in the casinos and keeping careful records. (See "The Professional Video Poker Player" on page 16 for more information.)

6. *The vulture.* These players may consider themselves to be pros, but their modus operandi is anything but professional because their actions often cause good opportunities to cease to exist. Instead of spreading their play around to realize a regular income, they take advantage of short-term opportunities created by the recreational players, in effect robbing them of jackpots they have built. The classic example of this kind of player came when the Flush Attack game was new and the machines were linked together, usually in banks of ten or more. These players would sit at a machine playing very slowly or just pretending to play while the unsuspecting tourists and novices played the other machines in the bank. Attack mode would appear on all machines when a total of three flushes had been hit on the bank, and the next flush would then pay 125-for-5 instead of 25-for-5. The vultures would then play as fast as possible, following a strategy geared specifically to the high flush payoff. As soon as anyone hit a flush, thus turning Attack mode off, they went back to idle mode and waited for their next attack. These players nearly killed the goose that lays our golden egg until the manufacturer (Sigma) modified the game to make it far less vulnerable to such tactics.

7. *The compulsive gambler.* This player may also fall at least partially into any of the above categories, but he lacks the discipline to play only the good games and/or to limit his play according to his bankroll. He may or may not have read a good book on video poker, but even if he has he often makes "hunch" plays instead of following the correct strategy. This self-destructive play may be reinforced by accepting the free alcoholic drinks offered

by most casinos. As with all compulsive gamblers, he will not stop until all his money is gone and he has dried up all sources of loans. Don't let yourself fall into this trap. (If you need help or know someone who does, Gamblers Anonymous is listed in the telephone book in many cities, or they can be reached at P.O. Box 17173, Los Angeles, CA 90017.)

In summary. Most of the serious readers of this book will become skilled players and be able to realize at least a small profit while having a lot of fun, eating free meals and, if from out of town, staying in good hotel rooms at very low rates. Many will become semi-professionals, and a few may advance to the professional level. The less serious readers will continue to play hunches and continue to be losers.

The Professional Video Poker Player

Yes, it really is possible to make a living playing video poker, and there are perhaps a couple hundred people who do just that. Many of them play exclusively in southern Nevada because this area is rife with high-paying games and attractive promotions. But high-paying games and promotions frequently show up in unexpected places all over the country, and a few pros travel to take advantage of these opportunities, especially since there are very few skilled players to burn out the specials.

Some books will tell you that the big money is made on progressives — that is, the pros just watch the counters on various banks of machines with progressive jackpots and jump on one when the meter is high enough to give them whatever hourly expectation they consider necessary to make it worth their time. While this was generally true in the early days of video poker when there were no "flat top" (non-progressive) games known to be over 100% payback, it is simply no longer the case. Oh, they still watch the progressives, but that's only for an occasional shot, and some pros pass them by because they know that the volatility is too great for their bankroll. The big money now comes from solid play on games that are over 100%, and even more so from the promotions that sometimes push the payback beyond 100% even excluding the royal flush.

Before you decide to become a pro there are many things you should consider. We'll look at some of those later, but first let's see just what the potential may be for you. To start with a simple example, suppose you're playing 600 hands per hour on a five-coin

$1 Deuces Wild at 100.75% average payback. At five dollars per play, you're wagering $3,000 per hour. Over the long term, you can expect to gain an average of .75% of your wagers, or $22.50 per hour, plus any slot club and comp benefits.

This example shows an expected average hourly win rate of four and a half times your bet on this particular game. Compare this with expert blackjack counters or poker players where the expectation is to win perhaps one maximum bet per hour. Of course it's hard work being a professional blackjack or poker player, and card counters often get barred from a casino's blackjack tables, especially if they don't have a good "casino act." Although slot teams have sometimes been barred from playing, it has been quite rare for a lone video poker player to be "86'd" because he or she was too good or was winning too much. Several times, however, I have seen the payoff schedule cut on a whole bank of machines due to professional play. On the flip side, however, bankroll fluctuations are generally bigger playing video poker than for blackjack. Poker is probably somewhere in between.

It would be nice if we could expect to gain $180 in each eight-hour session, but of course it won't happen like that. Video poker is a very volatile game. By that, I mean that it can cause very large bankroll fluctuations in the short-to-medium term (see "The Long Term — The Wild Ride" on page 56). Eight hours at 600 plays per hour is only 4,800 plays, which is far short of the long term by anyone's definition. But if you played eight hours a day, five days a week, the fluctuations should average out over a few months. The million or more hands played in a year would provide ample opportunity to realize your expected profit, give or take a couple of royals. Or to put it another way for the mathematically inclined, the more hands you play, the closer together the standard deviation curves get, relative to the number of bets.

This is not a recommendation that you quit your job to play video poker. Even if you do manage to win regularly, there's a certain moral issue involved. Gambling is a nonproductive endeavor; it often leaves some people with an unfulfilled desire to be creative. Also, it can become quite boring and perhaps hazardous to your health to sit on a stool and stare at a video screen all day. One known hazard is called Carpal Tunnel Syndrome; if your wrists start to ache, or if your fingers get numb or tingle, you should ask your doctor about this.

So just what does it take to succeed as a professional video poker player? The following attributes were described by Doug Reul, associate editor of *Video Poker Times* and himself a professional player, as the most desirable attributes for a would-be pro. (The footnotes are my added comments.)

1. First and foremost, you must enjoy playing the games. If not, you will soon grow tired of playing no matter how much money you are making. Of course you probably wouldn't be reading this if you didn't like playing, but you must be able to continue playing even when losing, comfortable in the knowledge that the odds are in your favor and you expect to be a winner in the long run.

2. You must be able to recognize hands and card combinations quickly. This can be learned by most people through practice, but it is better if it comes naturally because you will still be able to play accurately even when you're tired.

3. You must learn an accurate strategy for whatever game you are playing, and you must follow it carefully. In some cases, the strategy should be modified slightly to best take advantage of a promotion or a progressive jackpot, but you should never play "hunches." Intuitive play is *not* winning play.

4. You must be able to analyze a casino promotion and determine the value that it adds to a game. Games can be analyzed with commercially available computer software, and this has already been done for you for many attractive games, but it takes a lot of hand work to turn an analysis into a playing strategy.[5] Promotions, however, are sometimes difficult to analyze, and they are more and more becoming a necessity in order to realize a good return.

5. You should be able to achieve a virtually error-free rate of play of one thousand hands per hour. To accomplish this requires the manual and visual dexterity and the willingness to play two machines simultaneously, which will increase your return up to fifty percent over the long run. Most casinos permit this, and even

---

[5]*Video Poker Times* provides accurate analyses and playing strategies for many attractive games soon after they become available. Also from time to time it tells you how to evaluate new types of promotions. See Appendix E on page 180 for more information.

$5 Blackjack
Match Play!

Match Play Up To $5
On Any Blackjack Bet!

Present this coupon at any Station Casino Blackjack table prior to the start of a game and we'll match your bet of $5 for one play only, win or lose (pushes play again). One coupon per person. Cannot be redeemed for cash. Management has the right to change or cancel this offer at any time. Must be 21 or older to redeem. This coupon is valid at any Station Casino. **Expires July 31, 2001.** Settle to: BJ-STCI #1.

Palace Station	Boulder Station	Texas Station	Sunset Station	Santa Fe Station
Sahara &	Boulder Hwy. at	N. Rancho &	Sunset Road at	US 95 at
I-15	Desert Inn & I-515	Lake Mead	US 93/95	N. Rancho
367-2411	432-7777	631-1000	547-7777	658-4900

* 0 0 0 3 5 1 5 0 7 0 0 0 0 0 0 0 0 0 *

$5 Blackjack Match Play!

Up To $5 VALUE

Match Play Up To $5 On Any Blackjack Bet In July!

PALACE STATION
HOTEL · CASINO

BOULDER STATION
HOTEL · CASINO

TEXAS STATION
Gambling Hall & Hotel

SUNSET STATION
HOTEL · CASINO

SANTA FE STATION
HOTEL · CASINO

See Reverse Side For Other Details

when they have signs saying one machine per person you will rarely be asked to give up a machine. There is an unwritten agreement among pros that one will not ask another to give up a machine if he or she is actively playing two.[6]

6. You must be able to play at least eight hours per day, winning or losing, with only short breaks. You might play as many as 250,000 hands per month or about three million hands per year.[7]

7. You must be able to get along with other professional players. Information is everything in this business. If the other pros dislike or distrust you, or if you don't share information with them, you will not learn about many of the best opportunities.

Before quitting your regular job, you should have a bankroll sufficient to pay all your bills and living expenses for at least six months, *plus* a gambling bankroll that can withstand the very large fluctuations inherently associated with nearly all games of chance. The suggested minimum for such a bankroll is enough for a 99% chance of hitting a natural royal flush. If your choice of machines is the standard full-pay $1 Deuces Wild, this would be about $12,000 (see Table 6 on page 166). But even this is no guarantee of success. I know of one "professional" who lost a $20,000 bankroll in six months of playing $1 Deuces Wild. (We'll discuss the risk in an upcoming chapter.).

However, you don't need to be a professional to enjoy video poker as a recreation and to expect at least a small gain along the way. You have a respectable chance of winning on a modest bankroll provided you stick with the recommended games, play them accurately, and keep your level of play in line with your bankroll.

Of course, one alternative is to join a slot team. In this case you would be playing someone else's money. Typically, as a member of a slot team, you would be paid a nominal hourly stipend plus a small percentage of any large jackpots you hit. This is not a way

---

[6]But if you are asked to give up one of your machines, it's a good idea to do so without an argument. You don't want to draw too much attention to yourself. To minimize delays and hassle, you might want to ask the incoming player to buy your credits, but in some casinos this raises a red flag that you may be a pro.

[7]That's at least 3,000 hours of play a year, or half again as much time as most hourly jobs. Gambling is a tough way to make an easy living.

to get rich, and it's not as much fun since you won't get to keep the jackpot if you hit it, but it does insulate you from the bankroll fluctuations so it might be a practical way to pay your bills if you're retired or between jobs. Agree beforehand whether you get to use your own slot club card or if you must use the bankroller's card.If there is a cash rebate, one possibility would be for you to keep the rebate instead of being paid an hourly rate.

In any case, whether you are playing video poker or any other game, the IRS will be interested in your gambling income. Since any slot or video game jackpot of $1,200 or more will require identification for a form W-2G gambling winnings report, be sure to keep good records of all wins and losses for your tax return. At the time this book is being written you are allowed to deduct gambling losses up to the amount of gambling wins if you itemize your return. This might become a somewhat sticky situation if you hit a jackpot over $1,200 when playing on a slot team; you may have to sign the W-2G even though you don't get to keep the money. See "IRS Reports and Tax Records" on page 141 and ask your accountant or attorney for more specific tax advice.

Chapter 2

A Closer Look

What Does 'Expected Value' Really Mean?

"All professional gamblers rate games according to the 'expected value.' This concept, in fact, is so important to gamblers that, as with Yahweh of old, you rarely hear the words spoken — just the initials EV. No professional would ever place a bet on any game if he or she didn't think that the EV was positive." [Arnold "The Bishop" Snyder, *Card Player* magazine, January 23, 1998.]

Although "Bishop" Snyder writes mostly about blackjack, the entire article from which the above quote is extracted should be read by all serious players of any game, but it is especially pertinent to us because video poker is one of the few games where the EV can be precisely determined and you can get an advantage over the game.

But just what is expected value?

To put it in as simple terms as possible, the EV of any chance event is the average of all possible outcomes. But now we must define the word "average" which to a statistician may have any of several meanings depending on the context and the question to be investigated. In this case it is a weighted mean, computed by multiplying the probability of each possible outcome by its value (payoff per unit bet) and summing the products. Now let's see how to determine the EV of one video poker play.

For any dealt five-card hand, there are thirty-two possible ways to play it. You can hold all five cards (That's one way.); you can hold four cards and draw one (Obviously there are five possible one-card discards.); you can hold two cards and draw three (There are ten possible combinations for a two-card discard.); you can hold three cards and draw two (again ten possibilities); you can hold one card and draw four (There are five ways to hold just one card.); or you can discard all five cards. In any case, you have seen five of the 52 cards in the deck, so the draw must come from the remaining 47 unseen cards.

For each of these 32 ways of playing a hand, there may be many possible outcomes. Let's look at just a few of the possible ways of playing the following 9/6 Jacks-or-Better hand:

K♥ Q♠ J♥ 10♥ 4♥

Draw 1: Hold K-Q-J-10, hoping for a straight. Any ace or nine will make a straight, which pays 4-for-1, and there are eight such cards in the deck. But that's not all. Any king, queen or jack will make a high pair, which pays 1-for-1, and there are a total of nine such cards remaining in the deck. Since the other 30 of the 47 possible outcomes result in no payoff, the expected value can be computed as:

$$\frac{8}{47} \times 4 + \frac{9}{47} \times 1 = \frac{32 + 9}{47} = 0.8723$$

Draw 2: Hold K-J-10-4 (all hearts), hoping for a flush. Any heart will make a flush which pays 6-for-1, and there are nine such cards remaining in the deck. Also, any king or jack will make a high pair which pays 1-for-1, and there are six such cards available. That's a total expected value of:

$$\frac{9 \times 6 + 6 \times 1}{47} = 1.2766$$

Draw 3: Hold K-J-10 (all hearts), hoping for a royal flush. This is more complicated because you are drawing two cards instead of one. Since there are 1,081 possible outcomes instead of just 47, I'll skip part of the mathematics. Obviously there is only one possible way to make a royal (by drawing the ace and queen of hearts) which pays 800-for-1 (assuming five-coin play and a 4,000-coin royal). There is also just one way to make a straight flush (by drawing the queen and nine of hearts) which pays 50-for-1. There are 34 ways to draw two hearts other than A-Q or Q-9 to make a flush which pays 6-for-1, 22 ways to draw an A-Q or Q-9 (not both hearts) to make a straight which pays 4-for-1, nine ways to draw a pair of kings, jacks or tens to make three of a kind which pays 3-for-1, 27 ways to make two pair (e.g., by catching a king and a ten) which pays 2-for-1, and 237 ways to make a high pair (by catching just one king or one jack or a pair of aces or queens) which returns your bet. Thus, the expected value is computed as:

$$\frac{1 \times 800 + 1 \times 50 + 34 \times 6 + 22 \times 4 + 9 \times 3 + 27 \times 2 + 237 \times 1}{1081} = 1.3506$$

Therefore, if you were dealt this same hand many times and always drew for the straight, you could expect an average return of only a little over 87¢ for each dollar bet. Understanding this, you can easily see that you would be losing money on the play. However, if you always drew for the flush you could expect an average return of $1.27, and if you always drew for the royal you could expect an average return of $1.35 for each dollar bet. Which way do you think the hand should be played?

Note that in each case we are usually hoping for one particular final hand, but part of the expected value (sometimes most of it) comes from other possible outcomes. In draw No. 3, for example, nearly half of the expected value comes from final hands other than a royal flush. This is good because it reduces the volatility (bankroll fluctuations) of the game.

There are 29 other ways to play this hand, but these three give the highest expected values. If we were building a hand-rank table, we now know that a three-card royal flush (abbreviated RF 3) is generally higher than a four-card flush (Flush 4), which in turn is higher than an open-ended four-card straight draw (Straight 4).

The Volatility Index

When selecting a game to play, you pay special attention to the total payback. However, your potential bankroll fluctuations may be an even more important consideration, especially if you are on limited funds. But just how large are the fluctuations likely to be? The best mathematical model that I have seen is the standard deviation per unit bet, which Doug Reul calls the *Volatility Index*.

Don't let the complicated-looking formula scare you away from this concept. The Volatility Index is a useful tool for all players, and it may be even more important for recreational players than for professionals. You can skip the math and just use Table 9 on page 170, but it may not mean much unless you at least read the text of this section.

The formula for the Volatility Index (VI) is:

$$VI = \sqrt{\sum_i P_i \times (V_i - 1)^2}$$

where V_i is the value (per-coin payoff) for each final hand in the game's payoff schedule (including the no pay "zilch" hands), and

P_i is the probability of occurrence corresponding to each of those values.

Given any game's final hand payoffs and probabilities, you can calculate the Volatility Index yourself with only a pocket calculator. This may look difficult if you've never had a course in algebra, but actually it's very easy. Just follow this step-by-step procedure:

1. Find a table of final hand payoffs and probabilities for the game under consideration. These V_i and P_i values for various games can be found in Tables 2 through 5 in Appendix B on page 157 and in other publications. Also, they can be calculated by commercially available computer programs such as *Video Poker Tutor*.

2. Using a pocket calculator, enter one final hand's per-coin payoff (V_i), subtract one, and square the result (multiply it by itself, usually by simply pressing the "X" key followed by the "=" key). Then multiply by the probability of that final hand (P_i). For example, look at the Flush in Case 1 on the next page. Its payoff (V_i) is 7, so we compute $(7–1)^2 = 36$ and multiply by the corresponding probability (P_i) of .01469, which gives .5288 that you see in the last column.

3. Repeat step 2 for each final hand type. Be sure to include the Zilch hands, but remember that $(0–1)^2 = 1$ so the number in the last column will simply equal the probability of a Zilch final hand.

4. Total the last column. (That's what the Σ symbol means in the formula.) If you press the MC (memory clear) key before starting and then the M+ key at the end of step 2 for each hand type, this is already done for you; just press the RM (recall memory) key to get the total.

5. Take the square root of that sum (just press that $\sqrt{}$ key you may never have used before for any practical purpose).

You may wonder why the zilch hands have an affect on the VI while the "Bet Returned" hands have none. Think about it. If every hand resulted in a pair of jacks, your bankroll would never vary, and the VI would rightfully be zero.

Let's take two case studies and compare their Volatility Indices.

Case #1: One of the better flat top (non-progressive) games is the 9/7 Jacks-or-Better currently offered at the Stratosphere in Las Vegas. Here are the payoffs for that game and the final hand probabilities with perfect play.

Final Hand	V_i	P_i	$P_i \times (V_i-1)^2$
Royal Flush	800	.0000209	13.3330
Straight Flush	50	.0001102	0.2646
Four-of-a-Kind	25	.002346	1.3513
Full House	9	.01140	0.7298
Flush	7	.01469	0.5288
Straight	4	.01091	0.0982
Three-of-a-Kind	3	.07348	0.2939
Two Pair	2	.1275	0.1275
Pair of Jacks or better	1	.2027	0.0000
Zilch	0	.5569	0.5569

If you multiply each probability by its corresponding payoff and sum those products, you will find that the total long-term payback with perfect play is about 1.0078 or 100.78% while the VI (the square root of the sum of the last column) is 4.16. If you compare this with other games, you will see that this is a relatively low VI.

A lower VI is generally preferred since it means you will have smaller bankroll fluctuations. In this case, you can expect a standard deviation of 4.16 bets per play. On a five-coin 25-cent machine that would be 4.16 x $1.25 = $5.20. Of course you can't have a negative fluctuation of $5.20 on one play since you bet only $1.25, but you can have a wide variety of positive fluctuations. $5.20 is simply the weighted average of all fluctuations, both positive and negative.

Case #2: Another of the higher paying flat top games is the 15/10 "Loose Deuces" with a payback of about 100.95%. Its payoffs and final hand probabilities with perfect play are shown on the next page.

Final Hand	V_i	P_i	$P_i \times (V_i-1)^2$
Royal Flush	800	.0000221	14.1130
Four Deuces	500	.0002127	52.9508
Wild Royal	25	.001699	0.9785
5 of a Kind	15	.003171	0.6216
Straight Flush	10	.004354	0.3526
4 of a Kind	4	.06510	0.5859
Full House	3	.02114	0.0846
Flush	2	.01646	0.0165
Straight	2	.05541	0.0554
3 of a Kind	1	.2846	0.0000
Zilch	0	.5479	0.5479

The Volatility Index for this game computes to 8.38, which is more than twice that of Case No. 1. In other words, *we should expect bankroll fluctuation on this games to be twice as wide as for the 9/7 Jacks-or-Better in spite of the higher payback.* This is due to more than 10% of the payback being moved to the relatively infrequent four deuces hand.

So far we have ignored the value of a slot club. If this game were found in a casino that offered a 0.5% cash rebate, the total payback for Case 2 would be 101.45%.Since the slot club rebate is a fixed percentage of the bet, we could add .005 to each entry in the Payoff column (V_i) before doing our calculations. This would be more precise, but the VI calculation is not significantly affected, so it's not worth the bother.

The Volatility Index is a relative value; the greater the VI, the wider bankroll fluctuations you can expect when playing the game. See Table 9 on page 170 for the VI of selected games.

The Attractiveness Quotient

The Attractiveness Quotient (AQ) is a more general way of comparing games than any other measurement available, and it is well suited for use by the recreational player. It is computed by subtracting 100 from the total percentage payback to get the player's advantage, multiplying by 1,000, and dividing by the game's Volatility Index (see preceding page). The choice of 1,000 as a multiplier is purely arbitrary; its purpose is simply to scale the AQ into an easily-used range.

Note that subtracting 100 from the percentage payback of a game such as standard Jacks-or-Better yields a negative number (99.52 − 100 = −0.48), so the resulting AQ will be negative. This is because the player is playing against a house edge rather than having a positive advantage.

Taking the examples from the preceding section, we find that the AQ of the 9/7 Jacks-or-Better (assuming a humanly achievable payback of 100.78%) is

$$AQ = (100.78 - 100) \times \frac{1000}{4.16} = 188$$

Similarly, the AQ of the 15/10 Loose Deuces is about 113. In spite of this game's higher payback, its rather extreme volatility makes it less attractive for many recreational players. Of course some players like volatility; that is, they like the possibility of a moderately big win in a short session even though they're more likely to be a loser in any single session.

Any cash rebate from a slot club should be added to the Payback before calculating the AQ For example, it appears that the Stratosphere's slot club yields a .1% cash rebate on the high-paying games. This increases the AQ of those games to 212. Including a .5% cash rebate increases the Loose Deuces AQ to 173.

The AQ is a relative value; the more positive the AQ, the more attractive the machine for the recreational player. The AQ of selected games can be found in Table 9 on page 170.

Expected Value vs. Volatility

I have said that a professional player always holds the cards with the highest expected value, but there are exceptions — not many, mind you, but these should be considered. One is discussed in the strategy for Deuces Wild when dealt five-of-a-kind with three deuces. If the pair is threes through nines, then a slight gain in expected value can be achieved by holding only the deuces. In spite of this, some pros always hold the five of a kind. There are two reasons one might make such a decision.

First, it takes some time for the machine to pay out 1,000 quarters, and if there isn't an adjacent machine to play while waiting for that (and a likely need for a hopper fill) then the wasted time costs more in lost expected win rate than the slight gain on the play.

Second, holding the five-of-a-kind assures a payoff of fifteen bets, while holding only the deuces will most often end in a payoff of only five bets (for four-of-a-kind). You will get the fourth deuce for a 200-bet payoff only about once in 23 tries. That's trading a bird in the hand for a very volatile situation with only a tiny gain in EV.

Consider this as general advice, of course, because situations arise in other variations when it is actually recommended to hold only the deuces because a particular card with four deuces might offer a bonus.

There are many other situations in video poker where a close decision is a choice between a certain or very likely small payoff and an infrequent big payoff. For example, suppose you are playing Bonus Poker with a coupon that doubles the payoff for a royal flush, and you are dealt a pair of aces — but you also have three cards to a royal. Holding the aces guarantees at least getting your bet back, yet the draw for the royal has a higher EV. Your choice between the low volatility play and the higher expected value is a personal matter, and your current bankroll should be taken into consideration in this decision.

What Is A Penalty Card?

The term "penalty card" (or "interference card," which means the same thing) isn't used in the Precision Play rules, but it is used in the notes for the hand rank tables (Appendix B on page 157), and you will see it used frequently in more detailed strategies such as my pocket-size cue cards.

As explained at the beginning of this chapter, we often are drawing for a particular large hand, but much of the expected value of the draw comes from secondary payoffs. For example, suppose you are dealt:

K♥ Q♥ J♥ 4♥ 9♠

(not necessarily in that order, of course).

In most video poker games, the best play is to hold the K-Q-J of hearts, but we would make a royal flush only once out of 1,081 tries. On some of the other tries we may make a straight flush, a flush, a straight, three-of-a-kind, and so forth. These smaller payoffs make up a significant part of the total value of the draw, so anything that interferes with these secondary payoffs will reduce the expected value even though they don't affect the chances of making the big target hand.

So let's take another look at those two discards. The absence of the four of hearts from the remaining deck reduces the chances of making a flush, hence that card is called a flush penalty. Also, the nine of spades is called a straight penalty card because its loss reduces the chances of making a straight.

In some situations, the presence of a penalty card affects the EV enough to change the decision, but in most cases the difference is so small that it's not worth the bother for most players. If a strategy says "any penalty card" it means any flush penalty *or* any straight penalty.

What Does 'Optimum Play' Really Mean?

As we've indicated previously, video poker is a game of mathematics. The payoffs and probabilities remain constant during the play of any particular game. Therefore, there can be only one correct or "best" way to play a given game. Right? Well, yes, if you happen to have an unlimited bankroll and unlimited time, and you are able to play computer-perfect strategy. Unfortunately, we humans will have to settle for only near-perfect play on most of the attractive games, and we may even want to modify that if our time or bankroll is limited.

Many people say "optimum play" when they really mean "perfect play." In truth, except for a few of the simpler games, video poker is too complex for perfect play to be practical for most players. By perfect play, I mean that every play would be for the absolute highest expected value. It's true that there is only one perfect way to play, and if all decisions were as straightforward as in the example in "What Does 'Expected Value' Really Mean?" on page 21 then it would be easy to play perfectly.

In many cases, however, two or more possible ways of playing a hand have such close expected values that the discards may affect the decision (see "What Is A Penalty Card?" on page 28). Thus, the only way that perfect play would be possible on many of the games would be to take a computer to the casino and evaluate every dealt hand before selecting which cards to hold. This is illegal in Nevada and most other gaming jurisdictions, but even were it allowed, the reduction in your playing speed would cost much more than the slight gain in expected payback.

Many video poker games are so complex that no matter how many details are included in playing rules or how many notes are attached to a hand-rank table, it is nearly always possible to find yet another exception where a marginal decision is affected by the discards. So just how perfect is it desirable to make a playing strategy? In other words, what is optimum play?

What is "optimum" is actually a personal matter, depending upon your goals, bankroll, available playing time and skill level. For example, a playing strategy might be devised to:

1. Maximize the chances of a winning session,

2. Maximize the chances of a royal flush,

3. Maximize playing time on a given bankroll,

4. Maximize expected payback for money wagered, or

5. Maximize expected hourly win rate.

Let's look more closely at each of these possible goals.

1. Maximizing the chances of a winning session is the goal of many gambling "systems," especially progressive betting and money management systems. Although you might win in more playing sessions than you lose with such a system, the wins will generally be smaller and the losses larger than if you went for long term gain, thus actually increasing your net losses in the long run. This goal might be logical if you were going to play only one session in your lifetime, but for all practical purposes it is worthless (or worse).

2. Maximizing the chances of a royal flush might be understandable as a goal for a recreational player who makes only an occasional visit to a casino (or when playing in a tournament), but realistically it should be considered only in a situation where you have an unusually large bonus for a royal flush, such as a coupon or a short-term promotion that doubles the payoff for a royal, or a progressive jackpot that has reached a very high lev-

el. Even so, however, any strategy adjustments should be to minimize the cost of a royal, which is not quite the same thing. For example, it would be a rare situation indeed that would make it correct to break any made pay for a two-card royal flush. (But this and other such attempts at big payoffs might be correct for tournament play discussed beginning on page 114). If your goal is to hit a royal at all costs, then throw this book away and go for it, but be prepared for an extremely high net loss rate.

3. Maximizing playing time on a given bankroll may be desirable for a purely recreational player, especially if there are no games that offer over 100% payback. It is not a good goal for a serious player. An exception might be if you were playing mainly for fun and comps (as in Atlantic City), but in this case (since you're probably playing at less than 100% payback on the game itself) you probably should play for minimum loss rate, and this is almost identical to maximizing your win rate on a positive game.

4. Maximizing expected payback for money wagered is the "perfect" play discussed at the beginning of this section. Although perfect play is usually assumed for the purpose of computing the maximum payback of a game, it is seldom practical in the casino. For that reason, the paybacks claimed for my strategies are a few hundredths of one percent less than the computed maximum to allow for the difference between perfect play and practical human play.

5. Maximizing your average long-term expected hourly win rate (without overplaying your bankroll) should be the goal of all serious players, and the objective of this book is to teach you to be such an "optimum" player.

But even if you agree that your goal should be to maximize your expected win rate, the "optimum" strategy may not be the same for all players. Each individual has different abilities for strategy memorization, playing speed, duration of playing sessions, and so forth. Since perfect play is not practical or even possible on many games, each player ideally should have a strategy tailored specifically to his or her goals and abilities. I wish it were possible to offer each of you your own optimum strategy, but that would require intimate knowledge of your style and abilities. Unless you want to make your own adjustments you will have to chose from those presented.

Your expected hourly win rate is equal to the product of your advantage, your bet size and your playing speed. For example, if a game's payback as you currently play it is 100.61%, then your advantage is 0.61%, or .0061 as a decimal fraction. If you play this game on a five-coin quarter machine at 550 hands per hour then your expected average long-term win rate is .0061 x $1.25 x 550 = $4.19 per hour.

Now suppose you find a more precise strategy that will yield 100.63% payback from the same game if followed accurately. By necessity, that strategy will be more complex, so you probably won't play quite as fast, say 525 hands per hour. Assuming you master the intricacies of the new strategy, your expected average win rate is now .0063 x $1.25 x 525 = $4.13 per hour.

Thus, although your bankroll fluctuations will be slightly reduced, that "better" strategy not only is harder to use but also has cost you six cents per hour! What a wasted effort. Even worse, you may not have really mastered the new strategy, and although you make fewer errors, the ones you do make may be more expensive. Thus, the "more perfect" strategy may actually cost you money.

This same effect has been experienced by professional blackjack players, many of whom try different multilevel counting systems but almost invariably return to a simple single-level count for the best expected win rate over the long run. Even so, they don't all use the same strategy. There are several good single-level card counting systems for blackjack; some players also adjust for aces or have their own personal enhancements. Each expert uses the system that he has found works best for him. For each dealt situation in blackjack there is only one perfect way to play it, the same as for video poker, yet each pro uses what he has found to be his own optimum strategy. Thus the pro will not always make the perfect play, but the difference in EV between the perfect play and his decision will be very small.

In conclusion, there is no single optimum strategy for any complex game. For each game, the optimum strategy for each player is the one that yields the highest win rate for that individual without overplaying one's bankroll. Precision Play is an excellent compromise between simplicity and perfection and will thus yield a higher win rate than other strategies for most beginning to intermediate players.

Chapter 3

Precision Play

What Is Precision Play?

Precision Play is a computer-derived and player-proven technique for achieving the best win rate at certain video poker games. This was not the first book on video poker, and it obviously will not be the last, but it is the easiest to use without sacrificing expected win rate. For most players, Precision Play is optimum play.

Before Precision Play there were only hand rank tables, such as Tables 2 through 5 in Appendix B on page 157, and "guidelines" or "tips" that were often harder to follow than the Precision Play rules even though they fell far short of achieving any game's potential payback.

Some books and cue cards offer simplified strategies that are very costly in terms of payback. In others, the path to success is to memorize a table. Hand-rank tables work very well for many people — after they get some experience. But although you would be learning near-perfect strategy, your play might be slower, thus reducing your expected win rate even though you were making fewer errors in marginal decisions. Of course your accuracy and speed would both improve as you master the strategy, but why should you work so hard? Playing a game is supposed to be fun!

Precision Play is nearly as accurate as using tables, with the net loss generally less than .02%. Most players would lose more than that due to errors when following a hand-rank table.

You may wonder how I can claim that Precision Play will yield so close to a game's theoretical maximum payback when it is simplified for ease of use by a beginner. The answer is that the simplifications are on situations that occur very infrequently and where the difference in expected value between the computer-perfect play and the recommended play is very small. The total cost of such "errors" in the long run is very small (see "Errors in Precision Play?" on page 50 for more on this).

You have only a few simple rules to learn, and you will be a Precision player. You'll be playing faster, winning more (assuming you're playing a game that offers over 100% payback, or at least losing less if there are no high-paying machines available where you play), and having more fun. And isn't that what it's all about?

Precision Play vs. Expectancy Tables

To help clarify the advantages of Precision Play, let's suppose you are dealt

$$A♥ \quad K♦ \quad Q♦ \quad J♦ \quad J♠$$

(not necessarily in that order) on a full-pay (9/6) Jacks-or-Better with a flat 4,000-coin royal flush jackpot. You could hold all five cards, getting a payoff of 1.00 for the pair of jacks, but that's obviously not the best play.[10] Should you hold the four-card straight, the three-card royal, or just the pair of jacks? Or would you hold the ace "kicker" with the jacks? Each of these possibilities has to be analyzed individually against the potential long-term paybacks to find out which play is the best.

Table 2 tells us that the average EV of A-K-Q-J is .596, the suited K-Q-J (Royal Flush 3) is 1.401, and the pair of jacks is 1.537. (The tables give average EV because in any particular case the actual EV is affected by the discards.) Holding the ace kicker with the pair is not in the table because its EV is lower than for the pair alone at about 1.42. Note how holding a kicker costs you money.

The best play is the one with the highest EV, so the table indicates that we should hold only the pair of jacks. However, this does not take into account the affect of the discards. A computer run tells us that the actual Expected Values for this particular deal are .5745, 1.4708, 1.5365 and 1.4163, respectively, confirming that we should draw to the jacks even though K-Q-J is the best possible three-card royal draw.

---

[10]I could have said it's "intuitively obvious." That phrase always amuses me because of a math professor I had in college. He was explaining a derivation on the board when he said "The next step is intuitively obvious." Then he stepped back, looked at the board for a moment, picked up his books, and rushed out of the room. We sat there looking at each other. A few minutes later he returned and said "I was right. It is intuitively obvious." He then continued with the derivation.

Now, if the royal pays 4,700 coins, then the EV of the suited K-Q-J rises to 1.6004 while the others are unaffected, and on this payoff schedule, we should draw for the royal. The Precision Play rules tell you this, but hand-rank tables in some books don't always make a distinction. Also, if the cards were actually dealt in the order shown, then the K-Q-J happen to be in position for a possible sequential royal so we would draw to that if the game pays a sequential royal bonus.

In many cases, the Precision Play rules indicate variations dependent upon discards, the size of the jackpot, and so forth. Such variations are less easily expressed in a table format, usually requiring footnotes; hence the Precision Play rules are generally easier to follow than a table.

Another comparison occurs in Deuces Wild. Suppose you are dealt five-of-a-kind made up of three deuces and some other pair. Should you hold the made pay, which is worth 15-for-1, or should you draw to the three deuces in hope of hitting the 1,000-coin four deuces jackpot?

Another book's expectancy table gives the EV for three deuces as 14.9. Going by that alone, we would always hold the five-of-a-kind. Table 3 on page 162 gives the EV for three deuces as 15.026, suggesting that we should hold only the three deuces. Which is correct?

In a way, both are right. The other book's value is the approximate average for all three-deuce hands that are not dealt as five-of-a-kind, while Table 3 excludes only those quints where the pair is tens through aces. Why would I do that? It turns out that when we discard a low pair (threes through nines) the EV of the three deuces increases to 15.065.

If you think about it, you'll quickly see the reason for this increase. When a low pair is discarded, there are more high cards remaining in the deck, thus improving the chances of making a wild royal flush in the cases where we don't catch the fourth deuce.

For the highest expected value, we should hold the three-deuce quints if the pair is tens or higher but discard a pair lower than tens and draw to the three deuces. Yet the Precision Play rules tell you to always hold the five-of-a-kind. There's a good reason for doing this, which is further discussed in "Precision Play — Deuces Wild" on page 45.

The Payoff Schedule — Jacks-or-Better

Assuming that the cards are selected randomly (as mandated by Nevada gaming regulations), a game's potential long-term payback can be determined from its payoff schedule. Unlike the reel slots where we can't see all the symbols on each reel (and even if we could we have no way of knowing how many logical stops there are), this allows us to calculate precisely what to expect in the long run.

The table below shows the payoff for each final hand on a full-pay Jacks-or-Better machine, along with the probability of each occurring with perfect play, and its resulting long-term Average Payback. Any time I refer to Jacks-or-Better it is with this payoff schedule unless otherwise stated.

Expected Payback — Jacks-or-Better			
Type of Hand	**Payoff[1]**	**Probability[2]**	**AP[3]**
Royal flush	800	.0000248	.0198
Straight flush	50	.0001093	.0055
Four of a kind	25	.002363	.0591
Full house	9	.01151	.1036
Flush	6	.01102	.0661
Straight	4	.01123	.0449
Three of a kind	3	.07445	.2234
Two pair	2	.1293	.2586
Pair of jacks or better	1	.2146	.2146
Zilch	0	.5454	.0000
Total payback			0.9954[4]

Notes:
1. This is the basic full-pay schedule. Five coins must be bet to qualify for the 4,000 coin (800-for-1) jackpot on a royal flush.
2. Derived from the game analysis computer program.
3. Average Payback, calculated as payoff times probability. Each figure may be multiplied by 100 to convert to percent.
4. That is, 99.54%. Some machines pay 4700 coins (940-for-1) for a royal flush, thus increasing the total payback to 99.89%. Others may pay double or triple on a certain four-of-a-kind or offer other bonuses that increase the payback. See text for how to evaluate such bonuses.

At least one early book on video poker claimed 99.6% payback, and many other writers have apparently copied that figure. However, several independent analyses have shown that the *absolute maximum* payback with computer-perfect play is precisely 99.5439%.

These are the statistically-expected wins on a machine with the payoff schedule shown in the table. If you select such a machine and always make the optimum play, you will hold the house edge to less than one half of one percent. Of course this includes an occasional royal flush and your share of straight flushes. But the payback is nearly 97% even *ignoring* these big payoffs, or as good as the *total* payback (*including* the rare top jackpot) of most reel machines.

Except for the payoff tables (which depict the results of a computer analysis assuming perfect play), all figures given in this book assume Precision Play. Ironically, by often drawing to a royal flush when a higher EV play is available, less skillful players may hit more jackpots than we do, but along the way they will lose more in small payoffs. They can't possibly compensate for these small-payoff losses with the slightly increased frequency of a jackpot.

The full-pay Jacks-or-Better is most easily identified by the 9-for-1 payoff for a full house and the 6-for-1 payoff for the flush. (We refer to these as 9/6 machines.) Many machines pay 8- or 7-for-1 on a full house, and some pay as low as 6-for-1! Also, the payoff on a flush is commonly reduced to 5-for-1.

The most common short-pay machine has an 8/5 payoff schedule (where the payoff for a full house is 8-for-1 and the payoff for the flush is 5-for-1) with a 4,000 coin jackpot. (We refer to these as 8/5 machines.) From the table we see that shorting the full house and flush by one each costs about 1.15 + 1.10 = 2.25%, leaving a long-term payback of about 97.29%.

Other variations involve *increasing* certain payoffs but cutting the two-pair payoff to 1-for-1. This is even more devastating, as the cut on two pair costs nearly 13%. (There are a few games paying 1-for-1 on two pair that are attractive, such as Double Bonus Poker and Double Double Jackpot, but they are beyond the scope of this book.)

A few machines offer the 4,000-coin jackpot with only four coins bet, some five-coin machines pay 5,000 coins for a royal flush, and some three-coin $5 machines pay $15,000 for a royal. In any of these cases, this increase to 1,000-for-1 adds about one half of one percent for a long-term payback of just slightly over 100% (with the full-pay 9/6 schedule).

Some casinos feature added bonuses, such as paying double on four sevens. With unmodified Precision Play, about one in 13.44 quads will be four sevens, so this adds .0591 ÷ 13.44 = .0044 or about .44%. One casino even had some full-pay Jacks-or-Better games featuring triple pay on four sevens, promising 100.4% payback, but even this isn't enough to justify any deviation from standard Jacks-or-Better Precision Play strategy.

Why won't one set of quads in 13 be four sevens? There will be fewer low than high quads because we often draw to just one or two high cards but never to just one low card or two different-rank low cards. Also, when dealt a zilch hand, we discard five different *small* cards, and there are five chances in nine that one of them is a seven. One set of quads in 12.08 will be four jacks, and each of the higher ranks has about the same probability, so a double pay on any one of four jacks through four aces would add almost .5% to the payback.

The Payoff Schedule — Deuces Wild

With Precision Play, Deuces Wild offers 100.75% payback with just the basic 4,000-coin royal. This brings up a question — how do the casinos make a profit on such a game? The answer is that the vast majority of players rely on intuition and hunches when selecting which cards to hold, and they often hold a kicker (a non-matching card, usually an ace, sometimes held with a pair in live draw poker). Holding such a card is detrimental in any video poker game, but in Deuces Wild it's even more costly because it means one less chance of catching a deuce. Unskilled players make even more costly errors on Deuces Wild than they do on Jacks-or-Better.

The full-pay Deuces Wild can usually be recognized by its 5-for-1 payoff on four-of-a-kind as shown in the following table:

Expected Payback — Deuces Wild			
Type of Hand	Payoff[1]	Probability[2]	AP[3]
Royal flush (natural)	800	.0000221	.0177
Four deuces	200	.0002037	.0407
Royal flush (deuces)	25	.001795	.0449
Five of a kind	15	.003201	.0480
Straight flush	9	.004120	.0371
Four-of-a-kind	5	.06494	.3247
Full house	3	.02123	.0637
Flush	2	.01652	.0330
Straight	2	.05662	.1132
Three-of-a-kind	1	.2845	.2845
Zilch	0	.5468	.0000
Total payback			1.00764

Notes:
1. Per-coin payoff with maximum coins bet.
2. Derived from the game analysis computer program.
3. Average Payback, calculated as payoff times probability. Each figure may be multiplied by 100 to convert to percent.
4. That is, 100.76% long term expected payback with perfect play.

Any time I refer to Deuces Wild it is with this payoff schedule unless otherwise stated. Most short-pay machines pay only 4-for-1 on quads. Since quads account for nearly one-third of the total payback, we will not consider playing any such machine, even with a large progressive jackpot, except as specifically described later in this book. Some such machines may pay as much as 13- or 16-for-1 instead of 9-for-1 for a straight flush, but these increases fall far short of compensating for the loss of more than six percent when quads pays only 4-for-1.

Some casinos are more subtle, reducing the five-of-a-kind to 12-for-1 and the wild royal to 20-for-1. These changes reduce the payback to less than 100%, but it's not nearly as bad as the reduction on quads.

The expected long-term payback with perfect play on the full-pay game is 100.762%. However, the short-term payback (excluding four deuces and the natural royal flush) is only about 95% compared to almost 97% for Jacks-or-Better, so this game will cause larger bankroll fluctuations in spite of the higher long-term payback.

A few full-pay 25¢ Deuces Wild machines in downtown Las Vegas pay $1,175 for a royal flush, thus adding .31% to the long-term payback.

The Payoff Schedule —Joker Wild

Another game that promises over 100% payback is the full-pay Joker Wild that returns your bet on a pair of kings or aces. (Be extra careful when choosing a Joker Wild machine because even though some return your bet on a pair of kings or better, they often short the four-of-a-kind payoff down to 17-for-1 or 15-for-1 rather than 20-for-1.) Joker Wild is more difficult to play, partly because it has a longer payoff schedule as shown here:

Expected Payback — Joker Wild (Kings-or-Better)			
Type of Hand	**Payoff[1]**	**Probability [2]**	**AP [3]**
Royal flush (natural)	800	.0000242	.0194
Five-of-a-kind	200	.0000933	.0187
Royal flush (joker)	100	.000104	.0104
Straight flush	50	.000575	.0287
Four-of-a-kind	20	.00856	.1711
Full house	7	.01568	.1097
Flush	5	.01558	.0779
Straight	3	.01659	.0498
Three-of-a-kind	2	.1339	.2679
Two pair	1	.1109	.1109
Kings or better	1	.1420	.1420
Zilch	0	.5660	.0000
Total payback			1.0064 [4]

Notes:
1. Per coin payoff with maximum coins bet.
2. Derived from the game analysis computer program.
3. Average Payback, calculated as payoff times probability. Each figure may be multiplied by 100 to convert to percent.
4. That is, 100.64% long term expected payback with perfect play.

Any time I refer to Joker Wild it is with this payoff schedule unless otherwise stated. The total long-term payback with accurate play is over 100.6%. Excluding a joker royal or better, the medium-term payback is about 95.8%, so your bankroll fluctuations won't be quite as wide as for Deuces Wild.

A few full-pay Joker Wild machines pay $1,175 for a royal flush, thus adding .34% to the long-term payback. The bad news is that there are far fewer full-pay Joker Wild than Deuces Wild around.

For a while there were some very attractive Joker Wild (Two Pair or Better) available at 102% payback, but the strategy is different and quite complex. Unfortunately, they were hit hard by the pros, and the payoff schedule was changed. Surprisingly, this game has shown up sporadically in other casinos, usually for a very short time. If you want to be on the lookout for this opportunity, you should be armed with my cue card for this game.

Joker Wild seems to have reached the end of its evolution with the unattractive Deuces/Joker Wild and two moderately attractive versions of Double Joker Wild, but only time will tell. Although there are many new games appearing, most of them are either variations of Jacks-or-Better or Deuces Wild or else they are radically different such as Texas Hold'em or Double Down Stud.

Precision Play — Jacks-or-Better

Below is the Jacks-or-Better strategy the easy Precision way. Instead of memorizing a 37-entry table, you need learn only these eleven rules:

Precision Play Rules for Jacks-or-Better
1. Never break any made pay of two pair or better, except ... Break anything but a pat straight flush for any 4-card royal
2. Break a high pair only for a 4-card royal or any 4-card straight flush (including an inside draw); also for K-Q-J suited if a royal flush pays at least 4600 coins
3. Break a low pair only for K-Q-J-10, any 3-card royal flush, or any 4-flush or straight flush
4. Break a 4-flush or open-end straight only for a 3-card royal
5. If you have both a 4-flush and a 4-straight, go for the flush
6. Draw to any 3-card straight flush (even a double inside draw) unless it requires breaking a made pay, any pair, or any 4-flush or open-end straight, except draw to one or two high cards rather than a double inside straight flush with no high cards
7. Break A-K-Q-J only for suited Q-J or any three suited high cards
8. Break any three of A, K, Q and J for any two suited high cards
9. Hold an inside straight if it includes three high cards
10. Hold any one, two or three high cards, except ... discard ace from A-h-h (but keep A-h if suited) Note: "h" means any high card (J, Q, K or A)
11. Keep a suited ten when you have only one Q or J, and with a K if there is no suited discard; also, hold a suited ten with an ace if a royal flush pays 4700 coins and no discard is of the same suit

Always follow the *first* rule that applies to the hand you've been dealt. Of course, if you're dealt none of the hand types described, you must discard all five cards. Such a zilch hand will occur about three percent of the time, yet these five-card draws yield over one percent of the total payback.

Following this strategy will yield 99.53% long-term payback. That's less than .02% short of computer-perfect play. Although a "perfect" strategy has been published for *this* game, it is more complex. In any event, this strategy will yield the highest per-hour expected win rate for most players.

Precision Play — Deuces Wild

Many people find it easier to remember the following Precision Play rules for Deuces Wild because they are divided according to the number of deuces in the pre-draw hand. Remember to follow the first rule that applies to the hand you've been dealt.

Precision Play for Deuces Wild	
d*	**Draw to deuces alone except hold...**
4	All five cards (to minimize the chance of an error)
3	Wild royal flush Any five-of-a-kind
2	Any four-of-a-kind or better made pay Any 4-card Royal, or any suited connectors 6-7 or higher (i.e., any fully open-end straight-flush draw)
1	Any made pay, except always draw to any 4-card royal flush or fully open-end 4-card straight flush Any 4-card straight flush (including inside draws) Any 3-card royal (except ace high when one or more of the discards is of the same suit or is a ten or higher) Any two suited connectors 6-7 or higher
0	Any made pay, except always draw to a 4-card royal flush Any 4-card straight flush (including an inside draw) Any 3-card royal flush One pair (discard a second pair) Any 4-card flush or fully open-ended 4-card straight (note: Ace high or trey low is equivalent to an inside draw) Any 3-card straight flush (including all inside draws) J-10 suited Any 4-card inside straight except ace low Q-J or Q-10 suited K-Q, K-J or K-10 suited if no discard is of the same suit or is a nine or higher

*Number of Deuces

The prime rule in Deuces Wild is to *never* discard a deuce. While this may seem obvious, some people will discard the deuce from a one-deuce wild royal to draw for a natural royal flush. They will hit a jackpot this way an average of once in 47 tries, while three times in 47, another deuce will restore the wild royal, but the loss of the other 43 wild royals will cost much more than that one extra jackpot can ever make up for (the net average cost is nearly six bets). However, this applies only to standard Deuces Wild with a flat 4,000- or 4,700-coin royal flush jackpot. If there is a progressive jackpot or other bonus putting the royal over 5,400 coins it becomes correct to discard one deuce from a wild royal. It is also correct to discard one deuce from four or even three cards to a royal if a sequential royal flush pays a big bonus and the royal cards are in position for a possible sequential royal.

Due to the wild cards, there are more rules for Deuces Wild than for Jacks-or-Better. Even so, many people find it easier to learn these 19 rules than the 11 rules for Jacks-or-Better, probably because these rules are shorter and are organized by the number of deuces. Also, most people find it easier to learn these rules than to use a 51-entry hand-rank table.

Again, if you're dealt none of the hands listed, you must discard all five cards. This will happen over 19% of the time, which can make playing Deuces Wild somewhat frustrating, yet in the long run these zilch hands yield over 6% of the game's payback.

It might be helpful to note that you never hold exactly one card except a deuce, never hold exactly two cards unless it's a pair or a two-card royal draw, and never hold exactly three cards unless it's three-of-a-kind or a straight flush or royal draw. Of course you never hold just one nondeuce except when dealt four deuces.

You might wonder why a straight or straight flush draw with a high end lower than a seven is not considered open ended. Suppose you have one deuce with 5-6 suited. To complete the straight or straight flush on the low end would require 2-3-4, which would waste the deuce's value as a wild card. Similarly, holding 4-5-6 or 3-4-5 is comparable to an inside-straight draw.

Remember that high cards are no better than low cards except for royal flush draws. Middle-ranked cards (7–10) have the best straight potential. Since, of these, only a ten can make a royal, a ten is the best single card other than a deuce.

Lest someone chastise me for not mentioning it, I should point out that the EVs tell us to differentiate between high and low cards when dealt five-of-a-kind with three deuces. Breaking five-of-a-kind by discarding a small pair from three deuces increases the value from a made 15-for-1 to an expected value of 15.065. However, that's a gain of only .065 bets (about eight cents on a five-coin quarter machine), while if you draw two cards and hit the four deuces, it takes quite a while for the machine to drop a thousand coins (plus it often requires a fill). That time will cost more than eight cents in expected value due to lost playing time.[11] However, time is far less valuable if there is a neighboring machine that you can play while you wait.

Perhaps a more important consideration is bankroll fluctuation. You have been dealt a made payoff of fifteen bets. If you hold just the deuces, the payoff is more likely to drop to five bets (four-of-a-kind) than it is to improve. Therefore, when dealt five-of-a-kind consisting of three deuces and a small pair, my recommendation is to hold all five cards, especially if there is no neighboring machine to play while you wait or if you are on a short bankroll.

---

[11]Thanks to Bob Dancer for pointing this out.

Precision Play — Joker Wild

Unlike the other games that use a standard 52-card deck, Joker Wild adds the joker and deals from a 53-card deck. In live casino poker, the joker is usually a semiwild card, good only for aces, straights and flushes. In video poker, however, the joker is completely wild and substitutes for any needed card.

This variation spurred the players' interest and paved the way for other wild card games. It was probably predictable that Deuces Wild would become the most popular of the wild card games and lead to the most variations. Joker Wild and Deuces Wild have similar bankroll fluctuations, so the slightly higher payback and the excitement of the additional wild cards attracted more players to Deuces Wild. Deuces/Joker Wild followed, but its lower payback naturally limits its popularity. The latest entry is Double Joker Wild (slightly under 100%, but probably the highest paying game currently available in Atlantic City). There is also a rare Las Vegas version of Double Joker Wild that is over 100%.

The most common variation to Joker Wild is a reduced payoff on quads to 15-for-1. This costs 4.37%, reducing the total payback to just slightly over 96%. Needless to say (but I'll say it anyway), you should avoid any such short-pay machines. In some cases, other payoffs are increased slightly, but never nearly enough to compensate for this big cut on quads.

There are very few full-pay Joker Wild machines around, so its complex strategy is not worth learning unless you frequent a casino that has them.

The Precision Play strategy for Joker Wild below, which is for only the Kings-or-Better version previously described, is divided into predraw hand with or without the joker.

Precision Play for Joker Wild (Kings-or-Better)

Hands *with* the joker:

1. Never break a made pay of a full house or better

2. Break a made flush only for a 4-card royal or 4-card fully open-ended straight flush

3. Break three-of-a-kind for any 4-card straight flush (double inside only if it includes an ace or king; e.g., A-2-5-joker or K-Q-9-joker)

4. Break a pair of aces or kings for any 3-card or better straight flush (not double inside) or any 4-card flush

5. If you have anything less than trips, a 4-card straight or flush, a 3-card straight flush, or an ace or king, then hold a mid card (five through ten) with the joker (a ten is best)

6. If you have none of the above, draw to the joker alone

Hands *without* the joker:

1. Never break a made pay of two pair or better, except … break a flush for any 4-card royal draw, and break a straight for any 4-card straight flush or royal draw

2. Break a pair of aces or kings for a 3-card royal draw or better unless the RF3 includes an ace and not a king

3. Break a low pair for a 4-card flush or an open-ended 3-card straight flush

4. Break any pair for any 4-card straight flush

5. Hold any 4-card straight, or any 3-card straight flush

6. Hold A-K of same suit

7. Hold a king with any suited honor (K-Q, K-J or K-10)

8. Hold an ace with any suited honor if no discard is the same suit

9. Hold any ace, king, or ace-king combination

10. Hold any two suited honors (Q-J, Q-10 or J-10)

These rules are much more simplified than the Precision Play rules for the other games. Even so, they will yield about 100.6% payback, but you can get about 100.65% by following the hand rank table instead.

Errors in Precision Play?

There have been rumors to the effect that (horrors) there are errors in my Precision Play rules. Before these rumors spread too far, let me assure you that they are absolutely true! But just what do these "errors" mean to you?

First we must agree on just what comprises an error. The definition used for the above assertion is that any recommended play that doesn't always result in the absolute highest expected value is an error. Okay, suppose we accept that definition.

One example cited is my Jacks-or-Better rule No. 7, which reads in part "Break A-K-Q-J for suited Q-J or any three suited high cards..." No one argues with the "three suited high cards" part, but to make the perfect play when the queen and jack are suited but the ace and king are different suits, we must consider the fifth card. We know it's not a ten because rule No. 1 says to hold any made pay of two pair or better, so we would have held a made straight. We know it's not a high card because rule No. 2 places restrictions on breaking a high pair. We also know it's not a 9 or 8 suited with the Q-J because rule No. 6 says to draw to any three-card straight flush (even a double-inside draw). This leaves 30 possible fifth cards.

The worst error results if the fifth card is a 7 or lower that is suited with the Q-J. Suppose you are dealt A♦-K♥-Q♠-J♠-7♠. (It wouldn't change anything if the ace and king were suited with each other or if the seven was a lower spade.) *Video Poker Tutor* tells us that the EV when holding A-K-Q-J is 0.5957, and the EV of holding the Q-J alone is 0.5837, so my simplified rule costs .0120 bets, or one and a half cents on a $1.25 bet. Now you might consider this to be quite significant, but just how often does this occur?

Table 2 tells us that only 5,664 of the 2,598,960 possible predraw hands will be A-K-Q-J-x with no made pay or higher draw available. The Q-J will be suited in only one out of four of those, leaving 1,416 cases to be considered. An RF4 or RF3 has already been ruled out by higher rules, so the ace and king will both be of suits different from the Q-J in all of these cases. Thus, this decision occurs about once in 2,598,960 / 1,416 = 1,835 plays.

In only six out of 30 of those cases will the fifth card be a two through seven suited with the Q-J. That's one hand in 9,177 plays, or about once per 10 to 20 hours of play. At 600 hands per hour on a five-coin quarter machine, that figures to a net cost of about 0.098 cents per hour.

I don't consider a simplification that costs less than one tenth of one cent per hour to be an error. Sure, a professional video poker player may want to take this into account, primarily because he isn't likely to be playing this game at the quarter level. He probably wouldn't even be playing basic Jacks-or-Better at all unless there's a slot club rebate, promotion or progressive jackpot to boost the payback to at least the 101% level. A pro will encounter this decision a little more often, yet even on a five-coin $5 game at 1,000 hands per hour the cost of this error is still only about two cents per hour.

The only other case where it is better to hold A-K-Q-J is if the fifth card is a nine, in which case the EV when holding A-K-Q-J is still 0.5957, but the EV of holding the Q-J alone is 0.5935, a difference of only 0.0022 bets. Since this occurs in only three of the 30 cases, this is really in the noise level. When the fifth card is any of the other 21 cards, holding the Q-J is the best play, so this rule is correct.

There are other "errors" in the Precision Play rules with similar costs. If you're a pro playing high stakes, then such discrepancies might concern you. For most of us, however, complicating the rules with more penalty-card details would probably cost more in loss of speed than the potential gain.

Everyone seems to agree that the absolute maximum payback of basic 9/6 Jacks-or-Better is 99.5439%. Back in 1993, when I was still refining my Precision Play rules, I wrote a program to determine the payback of a game. Instead of assuming perfect play, I set it to calculate the payback by playing every possible predraw hand according to the Precision Play rules. This program determined the payback to be 99.492%, but there have been several refinements to the Precision Play rules since then.

After I posted an earlier version of this section of the book on Skip Hughes' video poker web site forum (http://www.vid-poker.com/), Jazbo Burns responded: "Dan, I input your strategy to my analyzer [and determined that] the EV for your strategy is

99.5348% — less than 0.01% from optimal. ... For the record, my basic (no penalty card) strategy is 99.5429%, which is within 0.001% of optimal. With the five (or seven, depending on how you count them) penalty-card rules I've given, optimal 9/6 Jacks or Better can be played." (By optimal, Jazbo means perfect play.)

Thus, according to Jazbo (whose web site address is http://www.jazbo.com), Precision Play for Jacks-or-Better will yield within .0091% of perfect play. At 600 hands per hour on a five-coin quarter machine, the sum total of all "errors" in Precision Play costs less than seven cents per hour. So is it desirable to learn perfect play? What if the more complex rules slow you down to, say, 580 hands per hour?

If you're playing this game at all, it's hopefully with side benefits that raise the total effective payback to over 100%. Let's suppose you are playing a five-coin $1 machine, and the side benefits are worth exactly one percent. Following the Precision Play rules (100.5348% payback) at 600 hands per hour, the game would yield an expected average win rate of $16.04 per hour, while perfect play (100.5439% payback) at 580 hands per hour would yield an expected average win rate of $15.77 per hour. At 590 hands per hour it would be a break-even situation, so you would have to maintain your original speed to realize a 27-cent-per-hour gain from perfect play.

Which is better? Which is easier? Whoa. Slow down. It's not that simple. This was only one example. A pro would hone his skills and be playing much faster, so his perspective might be quite different from mine. You should weigh all the factors before deciding which strategy best fits *your* skills and goals, but it is my opinion that Precision Play is optimum for most players.

I must again caution you that some writers use the term "optimum play" when they really mean perfect play. On most games, it's very difficult to achieve the indicated payback with only human play, but Precision Play will get you very close.

Chapter 4

The Short Term —Jacks-or-Better

This and the following sections will show how to determine your approximate chances of hitting a jackpot with a given starting bankroll. For now, we'll deal with short-term expectations, beginning with Jacks-or-Better. (If you're not interested in the mathematics you can skip these chapters and use Table 6 on page 166 to make a reasonable estimate.)

To begin the necessary calculations, let's start with $100 and play a common 25¢ 8/5 Jacks-or-Better machine. We'll call the lasting power of this bankroll the "short term." You'll soon see why $100 is considered only a short-term bankroll.

We always play five coins, so our wager will be $1.25 (playing fewer coins wouldn't affect these short-term payback calculations, but it would reduce the long-term payback because it doesn't qualify for the jackpot). Dividing $100 by $1.25, we find that we have enough for 80 plays. At odds of 40,000 to one we would seem to have only about one chance in five hundred of a jackpot, but this ignores the many small payoffs collected along the way.

Excluding the relatively infrequent hands of four-of-a-kind and better, the 8/5 game yields about 88.8% payback, so at the end of those eighty plays the small payoffs (on average) should be sufficient for another 80 x .888 = 71 more plays. After those 71 plays, we should have about 88.8% of 71, or enough for 63 more plays, and so on.

This is the beginning of a mathematical series which says that if we continue to feed this money back through the machine (or play credits) and fail to hit four-of-a-kind or better, our $100 bankroll will last an average of

$$\frac{80}{1 - 0.888} = 715 \text{ plays}$$

That's nearly nine times the number of plays made by feeding our ten rolls of quarters through only once.

But wait! Since four-of-a-kind should occur an average of once in every 424 plays, we can reasonably expect to hit quads once or twice in 715 plays, so it should not have been excluded. Restoring it to the calculation shows a short-term payback of 94.75%, so excluding only straight flushes and royals we find that our meager $100 should, on average, last about

$$\frac{80}{1 - 0.9475} = 1,520 \text{ plays}$$

so our small bankroll gives us better than one chance in six of hitting a straight flush for $62.50, and about one chance in 26 of a royal flush.

And better yet, on a full-pay (9/6) machine, the payback, excluding only straight flushes and royals, is 97%, so our $100 would last an average of

$$\frac{80}{1 - 0.97} = 2,665 \text{ plays}$$

thus giving us nearly one chance in three of a straight flush and one chance in fifteen of a royal!

A very significant conclusion can be drawn from this:

With a limited bankroll, the chance of hitting a royal flush on a full pay (9/6) Jacks-or-Better is nearly 75% better than on a similar 8/5 machine!

Isn't it worthwhile going out of your way to find and play only the full-pay machines? However, if you're stuck in a town with no full-pay games and intent on playing the machines, you're still better off on a 8/5 Jacks-or-Better than on most reel slots, but at least try to find a progressive with a high jackpot.

The Short Term — Deuces Wild

You may wish to refer to the preceding section for comparison as you read this because Deuces Wild is a whole different ball game when it comes to short-term expectations. Nearly four percent of its payback is concentrated in the four deuces minijackpot, which on average occurs only about once per 4,900 hands with optimum play, so we should expect larger bankroll fluctuations than on Jacks-or-Better. The frequency of occurrence of the straight flush and five-of-a-kind hands puts them in the short run, but the one-in-560 rate of the wild royal may put it in the medium term. Let's see.

We'll start with the same $100 as before, but this time on a full-pay 25¢ Deuces Wild (one with a payoff schedule as shown in "The Payoff Schedule — Deuces Wild"). Excluding the wild royal and bigger payoffs, the payback is about 90.42%, so our bankroll should yield about

$$\frac{80}{1 - 0.9042} = 835 \text{ plays}$$

Happily this is enough to expect at least one wild royal, so we can include it, making the short-term payback about 94.91%, so our $100 should last an average of about 1,572 plays.

This is a bit better than playing the 8/5 Jacks-or-Better, but it's far short of the expected occurrence rate of once in nearly 5,000 plays for four deuces, so that payoff must be considered medium term, which would require a bankroll of $300 to $500 for a reasonable expectation.

Note that the $100 starting bankroll provides about 40% fewer plays than it would on a 9/6 Jacks-or-Better. Therefore, the full-pay Jacks-or-Better may be a better choice for a player with a very limited bankroll in spite of the lower long-term payback.

The Short Term — Joker Wild and Other Games

Joker Wild offers the joker royal at 100-for-1 and five-of-a-kind at 200-for-1. Together, these two "minijackpots" should occur about as frequently as four deuces on the Deuces Wild. The short-term payback (everything up through a straight flush) is about 95.8%, so a small bankroll should produce slightly more plays than it would on Deuces Wild.

Most other variations are not nearly as attractive for a beginning or intermediate player as those recommended in this book. Even those variations that don't reduce the payback usually have moved some of the payback from the short term to the medium or long term, thus increasing bankroll fluctuations, often with little or no offsetting advantage.

But that's not to say that all new games must be avoided. Some variations that appear at first glance to be short pay surprise us and turn out to be even better in the long run than the standard full pay games. A few such variations are covered elsewhere in this book, and new ones are covered regularly in *Video Poker Times*. Strategy changes are required to take advantage of the variations, however, so you should not attempt to play an unknown game unless it's just for experimental reasons.

Even though the long-term payback may be higher, such games usually cause larger bankroll fluctuations. The casino still makes money on these machines because so many players don't know or don't bother to follow the correct strategy.

The Long Term — The Wild Ride

What can you expect in the long term? In a very general sense, that's probably the easiest question to answer about any game. Simply put, you can expect a gain equal to your action multiplied by your advantage (as you play the game). Of course if the game's payback is less than 100% then your "advantage" is negative, so although it's still possible to get lucky and win in the short term, you should expect a net loss in the long term.

First let's be sure we know just what is meant by "action," "advantage" and "the long term." Then we'll look at what we can expect along the way. "Action" is simply the total amount of money that you wager. For example, if you play 1,000 hands on a five-coin quarter machine, your action has been 1,000 x 5 x 25¢ = $1,250.

Your "advantage" is the amount you can expect to gain for each unit wagered, but the determination of your advantage is not quite as straightforward as for your action. The easiest way to show this is with an example.

The payback of full-pay Deuces Wild with Precision Play is about 100.75%. Suppose you are playing this game at a casino that offers a slot club with a cash rebate of two tenths of one percent.[12] The total payback is therefore 100.75% + 0.20% = 100.95%. Subtracting 100%, you find that your advantage is 0.95% or .0095.

Thus, in the long term, you can expect to gain .0095 times your action, so on that same 1,000 hands your expected gain is $1,250 x

---

[12]Most slot clubs pay a percentage of your action, but some pay on a percentage of your wins (payoffs). Since we are always playing games that are within a couple points of 100% payback either way, this makes very little difference in our calculations.

.0095 = $11.90 (note that I have rounded off to three significant figures).

If you are playing standard full-pay Jacks-or-Better in that same casino (with your slot club card in the reader, of course), then the total payback would be 99.53% + 0.20% = 99.73%. Subtracting 100%, your "advantage" is *minus* 0.27%, so on that same thousand hands you would expect to lose about $1,250 x .0027 = $3.38.

One thousand hands is really only short term (somewhere between one and three hours play for most players). Therefore, these *expected* wins or losses are only averages if you were to repeat the play many times. Now let's continue this discussion into the long term.

We'll start by converting the above figures to hourly rates. Also, since we're looking for winning situations, we'll consider only the Deuces Wild example. If your average playing speed is 500 hands per hour, then it would take you two hours to play 1,000 hands, so you would have an hourly win rate of half of $11.90, or $5.95 per hour.

Obviously you can't win exactly $5.95 on a quarter machine, but remember that this is a projected average. In any single session of only a few hours play it would be possible to lose several hundred dollars or to win several hundred (or even several thousand) dollars, but in any one short session you're more likely to be a loser than a winner.

I consider the long term to be at least 250,000 hands, which at 500 hands per hour would require 500 hours of play. If you average 20 hours of play per week, that's 25 weeks; so let's use six months as your "long term." In six months (26 weeks) at 20 hours per week, you would play about 26 x 20 x 500 = 260,000 hands. If all of that play took place on the Deuces Wild game discussed above, you would have an expected gain of 260,000 x $1.25 x .0095 = $3,090 (again rounding to three significant figures). And since this is the long term, you can reasonably expect to be within one or two royals either way of that figure.

What happens along the way to "the long term" is another story. Some professional blackjack players have likened their bankroll fluctuations to a roller coaster ride. There are large swings up and down, but with discipline and accurate play the trend is upward.

Video poker also has its ups and downs, but it is nowhere near as smooth as a roller coaster ride. The Stratosphere's Big Shot ride might be a better analogy. A glance at the payoff table for Deuces Wild shows that about 55% of your final hands will be losers and another 28% will be pushes (returning your wager), leaving only 17% of your plays to be true winners. In other words, ignoring the pushes, you will have more than three times as many losing hands as winning hands. (Assuming there is a slot club cash rebate, there is technically no such thing as a push. In the example given, the slot club turns a push on the game itself into a .2% win, which would amount to one fourth of one cent on a $1.25 bet.)

Excluding the royal flush and four deuces, the payback from all other hands is less than 95%. Thus, even on this game with over 100% payback, the trend is downward at about a five percent rate with an occasional sharp spike upward to the minus one percent trend line (when you hit four deuces) and the rare big spike upward to the plus .75% trend line when you hit a royal flush.

Yet another way to look at it is to figure the expected cost of a royal flush. Again using Deuces Wild for our example, we see that a royal is to be expected an average of only once per 45,300 hands, and you will be losing at about a one percent average rate until it comes. Playing that many hands without hitting a royal on a five-coin quarter machine, you would expect to lose about 45,300 x $1.25 x .01 = $566. If the royal happened to come right on schedule, that $1,000 "spike" would put you $434 ahead.

Chapter 5

The Benefit or Cost of Variations

Today, it seems as if new video poker games appear daily. While that statement is probably a gross exaggeration, new versions of the game do crop up more frequently now, and each new variation vies for the players' money with different enticements. Some of these don't last much past the "trial" stage due to very low payback or playing difficulty; after a brief try, most players avoid them. Occasionally a machine might fade away due to very high payback (e.g., over 102%) because the pros eat it up and the casinos remove it from their floors. Others survive either because of unique character or because the payback is still near or over 100%, or both. If you encounter a new variation, how can you determine whether its payback is sufficient to warrant giving it a try?

I will not attempt to cover broader variations such as Deuces/Joker Wild and Double Double Bonus Poker because the payback schedules make for even wider bankroll fluctuations than the games we have already covered, and the payback is usually well below 100%.

The tables in "The Payoff Schedule" sections show the probability of each final hand (assuming perfect play). To estimate the cost or benefit of a variation, it is necessary only to multiply the change in the payoff by the probability of occurrence and add the product to the total Average Payback. But note that the product is often a negative number because the payback has been reduced. Some examples will help to clarify the procedure.

Let's look first at the Jacks-or-Better payoff schedule. If the schedule is as shown in "The Payoff Schedule — Jacks-or-Better " except that the royal pays 4,700-for-5, what is the total payback? Well, that's 940-for-1, an increase of 140, which we multiply by the probability (.0000248), giving .00347, or about .35%. Adding this to the basic game's 99.54% payback with perfect play yields 99.89% payback. As usual, we must deduct about .02% for human play.

Another variation might be to reduce the full house to 8 but increase the flush to 7 (making it an 8/7 machine). If we subtract .01151 and add back .01102, we have a net reduction of .00049 or about .05%. This is a small loss, and we could probably recover most of that (or maybe even realize a net gain) with proper strategy modifications.

Another subtle change is to reduce the payoff on quads to 20 instead of 25-for-1. Multiplying the difference of five by the probability of .002363 reveals a very significant 1.18% reduction.

The Frontier on the Las Vegas Strip used to offer a bonus coupon when you cashed your paycheck. If you hit any four-of-a-kind on Jacks-or-Better with the coupon, the payoff was doubled, adding 5.91% for over 105.4% total payback! Due to a $100 limit, a dollar machine didn't give the full $125 double pay, but this still added 80% of 5.91% for an expectation of about 102% in the short term! (Unfortunately, this promotion was abused by locals running people through with phony paychecks, so it was finally cancelled.)

As we have noted before, a bonus on a certain set of quads, such as four sevens, must take into account the frequency of that particular final hand. We have seen that four sevens (or four deuces through four nines) will occur about once in every 13.44 sets of quads, but even assuming one in 13 or one in 14 would not cause too big an error for a quick approximation. In Joker Wild (kings or better), four deuces through four queens will occur with about equal frequency, and in Deuces Wild any set of quads (other than four deuces which is a separate category) will have about the same frequency of occurrence.

Another example is Tens-or-Better with the same payback schedule as Jacks-or-Better except that it pays only 1-for-1 on two pair. Returning the wager on a pair of tens adds about one fourth of .2146 (the Average Payback for a pair of jacks or better), or .0536. However, paying only 1-for-1 on two pair costs half of its EV of .2586, or .1293, for a net loss of .0757 or about 7.57%. As you can see, the cost of only returning your bet for two pair is devastating.

Sequential Royals

Some games offer a big bonus payoff on a royal flush if the cards are in sequence, thus the nomenclature "sequential royals." The most common sequential payoff is 50,000 coins instead of the usual 4,000-coin payoff when the royal is in sequence in either direction. This is currently being paid on certain games at several casinos in the Las Vegas area. This change in the royal payoff translates into $12,500 instead of $1,000 on a five-coin quarter machine for a 10-J-Q-K-A or A-K-Q-J-10 royal flush.

With no strategy changes, this adds approximately 0.38% to the payback of most nonwild-card games and a little less to wild card games. However, this is in the extreme long term. since only one royal in 60 will be in sequence (although optimum strategy modifications can increase this a bit).

At the time this is being written, the Fiesta in North Las Vegas is paying 60,000 coins ($15,000) for a sequential royal in either direction on a few games (up to 101.1% total payback). Also, the Santa Fe is paying $25,000 for a sequential royal (either direction) on some of their 25¢ Bonus Poker games (100.17% total payback). The Horseshoe (downtown Las Vegas) used to pay 100,000 coins ($25,000) on for a sequential royal (either direction) on all quarter machines, but as this is being written it has been taken off of all but a few games and may soon disappear altogether.

Some games (see "MegaPoker" on page 85) pay the big bonus on a sequential only in one direction. With no strategy changes, only one royal in 120 will be in the proper order. Talk about the long term — that's one in over 4.5 million hands!

When playing any of these games, I prefer to consider only the regular payback of the game, excluding the sequential royal. If it's an attractive game in that light, then I have a free shot at the big one.

Progressive Royals

Let's examine progressive Jacks-or-Better and determine what the royal flush jackpot must be in order to yield 100% payback. Most such games have a reduced payoff schedule so that a full house pays 8-for-1 and a flush pays 5-for-1. (This, as noted earlier, is called an 8/5 machine.) From the .9952 payback of a full-pay (9/6) game, we must subtract .0115 and .0110 for the reduced payoffs on a full house and flush respectively. (These numbers come from "The Payoff Schedule — Jacks-or-Better" on page 36) Also, since a royal pays the progressive jackpot instead of a fixed 4,000 coins, we'll deduct its standard .0198 payback. This leaves an average payback of .9529 from all hands other than a jackpot, so the jackpot must yield 1– .9529 = .0471 for 100% total long-term payback.

The average payback of any type of hand is equal to its payoff multiplied by the probability of its occurrence. With unchanged strategy, the probability of a royal flush on any one play is .0000248, so the formula:

$$\text{Average Payback} = \text{Payoff} \times \text{Probability}$$

for the royal flush becomes:

$$.0471 = \text{Jackpot} \times .0000248$$

and solving for the necessary Jackpot we get:

$$\text{Jackpot} = .0471 \div .0000248 = 1900$$

This is not a dollar amount; it is a multiple of the bet. Since you must bet five coins to qualify for the jackpot, the progressive jackpot on an 8/5 quarter machine must be 1,900 x $1.25, or about $2,375 for 100% payback. On a dollar machine the jackpot must be 1,900 x $5.00 = $9,500. You have probably already noticed that it's quite rare for a jackpot to make it to these levels.

Of course, we could be even more conservative and look for at least 102% payback. The jackpot must yield .020 more, so it must be .0671 ÷ .0000248 = 2706 (at least $3,382 on an 8/5 quarter machine or nearly $13,530 on an 8/5 dollar machine). It's extremely rare to find a machine where the jackpot has climbed this high, since a progressive jackpot that has reached twice its starting level usually attracts a flood of players until it is hit.

As the jackpot grows, the best play dictates drawing to the royal more frequently. Strategy adjustments for a progressive royal are beyond the scope of this book. If your interest lies in progressive jackpots, you should get a copy of Stanford Wong's *Professional Video Poker*. Ironically, making those strategy adjustments will reduce the short-term payback even as it slightly increases total long-term payback.

But don't despair; some casinos have full-pay (9/6) progressives. Such a 25¢ machine requires a jackpot of only $1,250 for 100% payback or $2,255 for 102% payback. It's very rare for a jackpot to reach $2,000, so if you find one and there's a seat available (and you have the necessary bankroll) sit down. It's a good opportunity.

Rather than cluttering up this text with all the mathematics or leaving you with myriad calculations to perform, Table 1 on page 158 lists the necessary jackpots for 100%, 102% and 105% expected long-term payback on various games.

But remember, you don't need a progressive jackpot for the payback to exceed 100%. For most people, Deuces Wild is the easiest game to play profitably, and many people consider it the most fun. Looking at Table 1 we see that standard Deuces Wild has the smallest jackpot requirement for 100% long-term payback. (These tables are based on 100.75% long-term payback on a non-progressive.) Table 6 on page 166 tells us that Deuces Wild requires only half the bankroll needed on a full-pay Jacks-or-Better machine for any given desired chance of hitting the jackpot, so our inclination may be to learn Precision Play on the Deuces Wild and stick to it. For many, that would probably be a good decision. Once you are comfortable with Precision Play, you can refine it by learning the complete hand-rank chart (Table 3 on page 162), but the additional gain is very small. Many people will lose more through errors and loss of speed than they gain through the more accurate strategy. (See "What Does 'Optimum Play' Really Mean?" on page 29 for more information on this effect.)

Jacks-or-Better, however, does not cause such large bankroll fluctuations, and a game paying extra on a flush or full house, or triple on four sevens, may even provide a similar long-term payback. The moral is to weigh all considerations before selecting a machine. (For a better way to compare machines, see the sections on the Volatility Index and Attractiveness Quotient and the summary in Table 9 on page 170.)

Table 6 tells us that the bankroll necessary on a ten-coin 5¢ 7/5 machine is only slightly less than on a 25¢ 9/6 machine. But why isn't it 60% less (the 50¢ bet is only 40% of the $1.25 bet on a five-coin quarter machine)? This is due to the reduced payoffs on the flush and full house. Since these hands make up a large part of your short-term payback, reducing their payoffs by a total of three units causes larger bankroll fluctuations. You will seldom find such a machine with a jackpot big enough to make it worthwhile.

Do Progressive Jackpots Reduce the House Edge?

Does an Average Payback exceeding 100% on a progressive jackpot mean that the casino is losing money on these machines? Of course not. Only a tiny percentage of the money wagered goes into the jackpot, leaving the casino with a positive edge even if everyone played perfectly (which they don't). Typically, about .1% to .5% of the action is added to the progressive jackpot, although I have seen games with multiple counters that put a total of one percent of the action into the counters.

Everyone who plays the game contributes a small portion of their money to the jackpot, but that doesn't mean that your expectations are adversely affected. You get a positive expectancy because of the people who have played the game and built up the jackpot, and because you are a Precision player. Unskilled players will continue to contribute to the jackpot and the casino's profit margin.

Double Progressives and Multiple Progressives

Some banks of machines are connected to two progressive counters but always pay the highest counter for a royal. When a jackpot is hit, the primary counter is paid; the backup counter then moves to the primary jackpot, the backup counter resets to its base value, and both continue to climb. In some cases the backup counter is shown, while in others it is not; this does not affect the expected payback at the moment, but being able to see the backup counter tells you ahead of time whether the game will still be worth playing after the jackpot is hit once.

Some (mostly older) individual machines have two progressive counters with an arrow that alternates between them with each coin or credit bet. If you happen to encounter one of these where one of the counters is high enough to make the game very attractive while the other is barely above its reset value, you may want to consider this tactic — play five coins if the arrow is currently on the low counter but only one coin if it is currently on the high counter. In either case the odd number of coins will leave the arrow on the other counter for the current play, so you are playing primarily for the big jackpot while conserving your money when the low jackpot is selected.

Another variation is a bank of machines with three or more progressive jackpots. One such example is a bank of Jacks-or-Better with separate progressives for the royal, straight flush, and quads. On some such machines you qualify for the jackpots with five coins, but others require six coins to qualify; the latter may appear to be full-pay (9/6) Jacks-or-Better, but the payoffs for a full house and lower top out at the five coin level!

Let's look at the six-coin version first. With all jackpots at their re-set levels of $2,125 for the royal, $325 for a straight flush and $46.25 for quads (I have actually seen such a bank of machines), the Average Paybacks would be as follows:

Typical Six-coin Triple Progressive			
Final hand	**Payoff**	**Probability**	**AP**
Royal flush	progressive $2,125.00+	.0000249	$.0529
Straight flush	progressive 325.00+	.0001053	.0342
Four-of-a-kind	progressive 46.25+	.002364	.1093
Full house	45 x .25 = 11.25	.01152	.1296
Flush	30 x .25 = 7.50	.01080	.0810
Straight	20 x .25 = 5.00	.01135	.0568
Three-of-a-kind	15 x .25 = 3.75	.07449	.2793
Two pair	10 x .25 = 2.50	.1294	.3235
Jacks or better	5 x .25 = 1.25	.2145	.2681

The total Average Payback (the sum of the AP column) is $1.34. Dividing by $1.50 (the six-coin bet) shows that the overall Average Payback when all jackpots are at their base levels is only 89%.

So how big do the jackpots have to be to exceed 100% payback? First we need a base figure. Ignoring the progressive jackpots, the short-term payback is $1.14 ÷ $1.50 = 76%. Dividing the neces-sary payoff for one percent payback ($1.50 ÷ 100 = $0.015) by the probability of a royal (.0000248), we find that the royal must pay $0.015 ÷ .0000248 = $602 to contribute one percent to the overall payback. Similarly, the straight flush and quads must pay $142 and $6.35, respectively, for each to contribute one percent to the total payback.

Now we can devise a formula to determine the total Average Pay-back at any given time:

$$\text{TotalAP} = \frac{\$RF}{\$602} + \frac{\$SF}{\$142} + \frac{\$Quads}{\$6.35} + 76\%$$

where, for example, $RF means the current dollar amount of the jackpot for the royal flush. Note that this formula is independent of the base reset levels of the jackpots.

Now let's look at a specific example. Suppose the current jackpots are: $RF = $2,900, $SF = $540 and $Quads = $100. Substituting these values into the above formula, we find that the game is marginally attractive:

$$\text{TotalAP} = \frac{2,900}{602} + \frac{540}{142} + \frac{100}{6.35} + 76 = 100.3\%$$

Note how big the jackpots must be to compensate for betting six coins when that sixth coin does not increase the payoffs on non-jackpot hands. Note also that the jackpot for quads is by far the most significant in determining whether the game is attractive. Increasing the jackpot for quads in the above example to $135 raises the total Average Payback to 105%, or over 102% in the short run (i.e., ignoring the straight flush and royal), making it quite attractive.

Now we'll look at the five-coin version. Of course, it's an 8/5 payoff schedule, and the jackpots typically reset to the standard full-pay levels. The Average Payback schedule looks like the table below, so it yields a short-term payback of $1.11 ÷ $1.25 = 88.8% as compared to only 76% for the six-coin version discussed above.

Typical Five-coin Triple Progressive				
Final hand	**Payoff**		**Probability**	**AP**
Royal flush	progressive	$1,000.00+	.0000249	$.0249
Straight flush	progressive	62.50+	.0001053	.0066
Four-of-a-kind	progressive	31.25+	.002364	.0739
Full house	40 x .25 =	10.00	.01152	.1152
Flush	25 x .25 =	6.25	.01080	.0675
Straight	20 x .25 =	5.00	.01135	.0568
Three-of-a-kind	15 x .25 =	3.75	.07449	.2793
Two pair	10 x .25 =	2.50	.1294	.3235
Jacks or better	5 x .25 =	1.25	.2145	.2681

The long-term payback with all counters at their reset values is 97.23%. Clearly, the 8/5 payoff schedule doesn't cut the payback or increase the volatility nearly as much as requiring a sixth coin which isn't reflected in the basic payoff schedule at all.

Dividing the necessary payoff for one percent payback ($0.0125) by each corresponding probability, we find that the royal, straight flush and quads must pay $502, $119 and $5.29, respectively, for each to contribute one percent to the payback.

Thus, the long-term Average Payback for a 25¢, five-coin, 8/5 triple progressive is approximately:

$$TotalAP = \frac{\$RF}{\$500} + \frac{\$SF}{\$120} + \frac{\$Quads}{\$5.30} + 88.8\%$$

If the royal flush is at $1,200, and the straight flush is at $100, then the jackpot for quads need only be $42 to yield 100% payback. A quads jackpot of $70 would typically yield over 105%. Of course this rate ends when anyone hits four-of-a-kind and the jackpot resets, regardless of whether it was you or someone else who hit it.

The Ramada Express in Laughlin used to pay triple on four sevens, plus the slot club's small cash rebate, together adding about .7% to the payback. They may sometimes still offer this bonus. When evaluating a machine, be sure to include *all* the variables in your calculations. (See "Aces & Eights" on page 74 for another attractive multiple progressive.)

Progressive Quads

It seems as if progressive jackpots on quads may be replacing the old standby progressive on royals to attract players to the short payback machines, and this may be the best thing that has happened to progressives in general. The quads jackpot grows faster than a royal jackpot in proportion to its reset value, so it more quickly contributes a meaningful addition to the payback.

Like the triple progressives previously discussed, these machines are typically found in banks of eight or more, and most have the five-coin, 8/5 payoff schedule.

Since quads occurs on average about once or twice per hour of play, it's possible to find machines offering over 100% payback in the short term. Unfortunately, this also means that if there are eight active players on the bank of machines, then it's likely that someone will hit quads within about five minutes, and there's only one chance in eight that it will be you.

We can determine from "The Payoff Schedule — Jacks-or-Better" on page 36 that when the quads jackpot is 125 coins, then the long-term payback of an 8/5 machine is only about 97.3%. However, quads accounts for over 5.9% of that, so if the jackpot on quads is at double the base level (i.e., 250 coins, or $62.50 on a 25¢ machine), we can add 5.9% to the base 97.3%, giving a total of 103.2%. Even ignoring the payoffs for a straight flush or royal, we have a potential 100.7% short-term payback!

For a quick estimate of the total payback, start with 100% when the quads jackpot is at 185 coins ($46 on a 25¢ machine) and add one percent for each 21 coins ($5.25) that the quads jackpot is above that level.

To determine the short-term payback (i.e., ignoring the straight flush and royal), subtract 245 instead of 185. For example, for a $75 jackpot (300 coins), subtract 245 from 300, and divide by 21, giving 2.6% positive expectancy in the *short term*.

In one casino I have seen such a setup with one progressive jackpot counter for four sevens and another for all other quads. You can quickly approximate the total payback as follows: Multiply the jackpot for all quads other than sevens by 13, and add the jackpot for four sevens. If it's a quarter machine, then divide the result by 75, or if it's a dollar machine, then divide by 300. This gives the total percent payback for quads. Add this to 91.6% (the 8/5 machine's payback excluding quads) to get total payback.

For example, suppose the jackpots on a 25¢ machine are at $114.25 (four sevens) and $57.50 (all other quads). Ignoring the cents, we find that (57 x 13 + 114) ÷ 75 + 91.6 = 103.0%. To get the short-term payback, subtract 2.5%, leaving about 100.5%. To get the short-term payback directly, add 89.1 instead of 91.6 in the formula.

When playing for a progressive quads jackpot on an 8/5 machine you should break a pat full house to draw to the trips if the quads jackpot is at least 5.5 times the base value of 125-for-5, and draw to a low pair in preference to a four-card flush if the quads jackpot is at least 3.5 times the base value. On a 9/6 machine the quads jackpot must be at least 6.1 times the base value to justify breaking a full house, and you should draw to a low pair in preference to a four-card flush only if the quads jackpot is at least 4.2 times the base value.

Sevens Wild (or Eights Wild)

Sevens Wild and Eights Wild machines may have the same payoff schedule as Deuces Wild, but even so the payback is nearly two percent lower because most straight draws and straight flush draws that would have been open-ended on Deuces Wild become inside draws.

For example, 8-9-10-J must be considered an inside draw since it requires a seven to complete it at the low end, thus wasting the value of the seven as a wild card, and 6-8-9-10 is equivalent to a double-inside draw. If this is confusing, consider this — given a fully open-ended straight draw such as 9-10-J-Q there are 12 cards that will complete the straight (any 8, K or wild 7). But there are only eight cards that will complete 3-4-5-6 or 8-9-10-J, and only four that will complete any of 4-5-6-8, 5-6-8-9 or 6-8-9-10.

When you hold one or more wild sevens, there are no fully open-ended straight flush draws. In Deuces Wild, 5-6-7-2 through 9-10-J-2 do not require a deuce (as a two) to complete the straight, so there are 20 cards that will make either a straight or straight flush. In Sevens Wild, however, there is no comparable draw. The 2-3-4 is not fully open-ended at the bottom; 3-4-5 requires a seven (as a seven) to complete it at the top end; and 9-10-J needs a seven at the bottom end, so there are only sixteen cards that will make a straight or straight flush in any of these cases.

The above discussion applies equally to Eights Wild, except that 3-4-5 with a wild 8 is fully open-ended. These games are not recommended, but they may be your best choice where they are full pay and there are no full-pay Deuces Wild available.

Bonus Deuces

When I first saw Bonus Deuces at Sam's Town with a payoff of only 4-for-1 for quads, I thought it was just another variation designed to entice unwary players away from the full-pay machines. Due to the low estimated payback, I offered only a few obvious changes to the standard Deuces Wild strategy. Many readers expressed an interest in this game, however, citing an article which projected a payback of up to 101.3%. As a result of this controversy, I did a complete analysis. The results surprised me. Here is the payoff schedule, along with final hand probabilities with perfect play:

Expected Payback — Bonus Deuces			
Type of Hand	Payoff[1]	Probability[2]	AP[3]
Royal flush (natural)	800	.00002254	.0180
Four deuces	400	.0002091	.0836
Royal flush (deuces)	20	.001666	.0333
Five of a kind	10	.003081	.0308
Straight flush	10	.004684	.0468
Four of a kind	4	.06257	.2503
Full house	4	.02617	.1047
Flush	3	.02010	.0603
Straight	2	.05583	.1117
Three of a kind	1	.2699	.2699
Zilch	0	.5557	.0000
Total payback			1.0093 [4]

Notes:
1. Five coins must be bet to win the jackpot on a natural royal or to get the double pay on four deuces.
2. Derived from the game analysis computer program.
3. Average Payback, calculated as payoff times probability.
4. That is, 100.93% long term expected payback with perfect play.

The complete analysis reveals that with Precision Play rules generated *specifically* for this game we can expect at least 100.9% payback, making it one of the highest payback fixed-jackpot games with more than just a few machines available.

You get the double pay on four deuces only if you play five coins. Playing fewer than maximum coins costs nearly 4.2% on the four deuces payoff and about one percent on the royal flush, thus reducing the total payback to less than 96%. Therefore, it is imperative that you do not play these machines unless you will be playing five coins every hand!

Bankroll fluctuations will be greater even than with regular Deuces Wild since more than ten percent of the payback is concentrated in the two jackpots. Similarly, the chances of a small win are reduced. The primary incentive for playing this game is having that $500 jackpot in the medium term (about once in 4,800 hands) as compared to the long term for the natural royal flush (a $1,000 jackpot averaging once in 45,000 hands).

For a serious player at 600 hands per hour, a .9% advantage translates to an expected gain of about $6.75 per hour. Too bad these machines are offered only in the 25¢ denomination.

Following is the complete Precision Play strategy for Bonus Deuces. Following these rules will yield very close to the maximum possible payback.

Precision Play Strategy for Bonus Deuces	
#d	**Draw to deuces alone except hold…**
4	Hold all five cards (to minimize the chance of an error)
3	Only the three deuces, discarding even a wild royal
2	Any 4-of-a-kind or better made pay Any 4-card royal flush

1	Any pat pay, except:
	    break a flush, straight, or three-of-a-kind for any 4-card royal;
	    break a straight for a 4-card straight flush (not double inside);
	    break three-of-a-kind for any 4-card straight flush draw
	Any 4-card straight flush (including inside draws)
	Any 3-card royal (except Ace high)
	Any two suited connectors 6-7 or higher

0	Any pat pay, except discard the nine from a king high straight flush, and go for the royal Any 4-card straight flush (including an inside draw) Any 3-card royal flush Any 4-card flush Two pair (yes, hold both pairs when dealt two pair) A 3-card open-ended straight flush One pair A 4-card open-end straight (not A-high or three-low) Any 3-card straight flush (even a double-inside draw) Any two suited high cards except ace-high (but not king high if any discard is the same suit) Any 4-card inside straight (but not A-3-4-5)
#d means number of deuces	

Bonus Sevens

There are also some Bonus Sevens machines mixed with the Bonus Deuces. Once again, we have to stress the importance of checking the kind of machine you're playing. Bonus Sevens and Bonus Deuces have the same payoff schedule except that on Bonus Sevens, a straight flush pays only 9-for-1 but five-of-a-kind pays 12-for-1. Nearly all straight and straight flush draws become inside draws due to the fact that the wild card is in the middle of the card sequence (see "Sevens Wild (or Eights Wild)" on page 69), but the number of five-of-a-kinds won't be diminished.

The net result is that the total payback is reduced more than one percent. Use the same strategy as for Bonus Deuces, but note that there is no such thing as a fully open-ended straight or straight flush draw when holding a seven. Therefore, don't hold those suited connectors with a wild card, and don't draw to an inside straight missing the seven. Better yet, stick with the Bonus Deuces.

Double Pay Deuces Wild

This is a much more common game than Bonus Deuces described on the preceding page, but it offers less than 100% payback. It's mentioned here only to point out the difference and recommend that you avoid it.

Double Bonus Poker

The full pay (10/7) version of Double Bonus Poker is one of the few Jacks or Better type of games that offers over 100 percent potential payback in spite of only returning the player's bet for two pair. It has been intentionally omitted from this book because it is rarely attractive for non-professional players who are looking for the best play for their money. I have three reasons for saying this: (1) The volatility (expected bankroll fluctuations) is even greater than for Deuces Wild, (2) the maximum payback is only marginally positive at 100.15% (about one-fifth the player advantage of Deuces Wild), and (3) the strategy is so complex that it can't be reduced to Precision Play rules, so many players will not achieve even 100 percent payback.

If you are seriously interested, this game is covered in *Video Poker Times* issue 3.2, and the 5-way progressive in issue 3.4, available for $6.00 each, postpaid. A pocket sized cue card (hand rank table) is also available (see page 183).

Loose Deuces and Triple Pay Deuces Wild

Other Deuces Wild variations pay 2500- or 3000-for-5 for four deuces. The payoff schedules are more closely related to the common short-pay Deuces Wild than to Bonus Deuces, as you will see in this comparison:

Final Hand	Prob*	Four Deuces payoff and its effect				
		1000	2500	Change	3000	Change
Royal flush (natural)	.0000221	800	800	.0000	800	.0000
Four deuces	.000213	200	500	+.0639	600	+.0852
Royal flush (wild)	.00170	25	25	.0000	20	−.0085
Five-of-a-kind	.00317	15	15	.0000	10	−.0159
Straight flush	.00435	9	10	+.0043	8	−.0043
Four-of-a-kind	.0651	5	4	−.0651	4	−.0651
Full house	.0211	3	3	.0000	3	.0000
Flush	.0165	2	2	.0000	2	.0000
Straight	.0554	2	2	.0000	2	.0000
Three-of-a-kind	.2846	1	1	.0000	1	.0000
Net change*				+0.0031		−0.0086
Standard full-pay Deuces Wild payback				+1.0075		+1.0075
Resulting approximate long-term payback*				1.01060		.9989

*Approximate, when following the Bonus Deuces playing strategy on the preceding page with the modifications described in the text below.

The surprising result is a long-term payback of about 101% on the 2500-coin Loose Deuces and nearly 99.9% on the 3000-coin Triple Pay game. (A more recent complete analysis puts the payback of the 15/10 Loose Deuces at 100.95%.) Thus the 15/10 Loose Deuces offers slightly higher payback than Bonus Deuces. But beware — nearly 12% of the payback is concentrated in the four deuces and royal jackpots, so very large bankroll fluctuations are to be expected and do occur. At 500 hands per hour, you have an expected *loss* rate of about $70 per hour while waiting for four deuces or a royal.

Loose Deuces will be attractive to some because of the $625 medium-term jackpot, and to others because of the high overall long-term payback. You should achieve fair results with the Bonus Deuces strategy, except don't hold two pair, and draw to one pair in preference to a four-card flush.

An even better version of Loose Deuces, paying 17-for-1 for five-of-a-kind, shows up occasionally but doesn't last long due to the high payback: about 101.6%. A cue card is available which is accurate for the 17/10, 15/10, and 15/8 versions (see Appendix E on page 180). The strategy for Loose Deuces is in *Video Poker Times* issue 3.1.

Aces & Eights

Circus Circus casino in Las Vegas has a bank of Aces & Eights in multiple progressives. Although this game is basically a 25¢ 8/5 Jacks-or-Better, it pays double (250-for-5) for four sevens and $100 for four aces or four eights, and there are two progressive jackpots: one starting at $1,000 for a royal flush, and one starting at $12,500 for a sequential royal.

With both progressives at their reset levels, the payback is as follows:

Aces and Eights Payback	
Basic 8/5 Jacks-or-Better	97.27%
Add for $62.50 on quad 7s	.44
Add for $100.00 on quad 8s	.96
Add for $100.00 on quad aces	1.10
Add for $12,500 for sequential royal	.38
Add for .5% slot club cash rebate	.50
Total payback	100.65%

As the progressive jackpots grow, add .1% for each increase of $50.20 above $1,000 for a royal flush or $3,012 above $12,500 for a sequential royal.

The strategy rules are for this game are fairly straightforward. Follow the standard Precision Play rules for Jacks-or-Better except watch for three-card sequential royal draws, which are worth more than a high pair or an inside straight flush draw.

Here's a trick you can use on many progressive machines — If you are dealt a pat jackpot hand, press all the Hold buttons but then check the size of the jackpot before pressing Draw. If it's just over its reset level, you have the option to wait for it to build up before pressing the Draw button to claim your payoff. Don't wait if it's already high, and don't wait too long in any case as many players tend to play faster when the jackpot is high.

Of course you will *never* play fewer than five coins since you will not qualify for any of the jackpots. Paying fewer than five coins reduces the payback to only about 96%. You will have larger bankroll fluctuations in the short-term due to the 8/5 payoff schedule, but the medium-term payback (everything less than a straight flush) is slightly better than for the standard 9/6 schedule, so you get this generous payback without serious bankroll fluctuations.

If you're on a limited gaming budget or just want to practice, there is also a small bank of 5¢ Aces & Eights. Just divide all the dollar amounts above by five.

A word of caution is necessary here because not all banks of these machines pay 400 coins for quad aces or eights. Check the payoff schedule before playing.

Other Variations

Watch for four-coin machines. These are sometimes full pay, but only four quarters need be played to qualify for the $1,000 jackpot. This 1,000-for-1 payoff raises the long-term payback to 100%, and playing four coins instead of five reduces the necessary bankroll for any desired chance at the jackpot by about 20%.

Dozens of other variations keep cropping up and vying for your quarters (and in some cases nickels and dollars). Most of these machines require strategy changes that would necessitate a whole new analysis; but why bother when history shows that these bonuses can't compensate for the reduced low end payoffs? The serious player will stick with the recommended full-pay machines.

The $5 and higher denominations often qualify for the jackpot with fewer than five coins played. As long as they are full pay, the Precision Play strategy is unchanged. To calculate the payback, it is necessary to convert the dollar amount of the jackpot to a number of coins of the size being bet, and divide by the number of coins required to qualify.

For example, suppose a three-coin $5 machine has a $15,000 jackpot. Dividing $15,000 by $5 shows that the jackpot is equal to 3,000 coins, and dividing that by the three coins required to qualify indicates a 1,000-for-1 payoff, yielding the same 100% long-term payback as the four-coin 25¢ machines. A slot club rebate could make this quite attractive, but again, no machine is attractive if your bankroll isn't strong enough to withstand the short-term fluctuations.

I was very pleasantly surprised by variations I call Super-Full-Pay at the Stratosphere. These are standard Jacks-or-Better machines but with the payoff increased by one for either the flush (9/7) or the full house (10/6). These are flat-top machines, of course (flat $1,000 jackpot for the royal flush), which would yield 99.5% payback with the standard 9/6 schedule. However, as you can see in "The Payoff Table — Jacks-or-Better," adding one to the full house (10/6) increases the payback by 1.15% to a total of 100.65%, putting it on a near par with Deuces Wild and making this the highest paying flat-top Jacks-or-Better around. No changes from standard Precision Play are required for optimum payback.

The 9/7 schedule adds 1.09% for a total of 100.59% when following standard Jacks-or-Better strategy. This can be increased to over 100.7% by some strategy changes, such as drawing to a three-card flush with two high cards in preference to the two-card royal. The complete strategy is available on a cue card.

It's your choice. With no strategy changes, the 10/6 has slightly higher payback, but bankroll fluctuations would be slightly smaller on the 9/7. I suggest these games in preference to Deuces Wild at nearly the same payback because of their much lower volatility.

The publicity was successful in attracting customers without costing the casino money. It is a documented fact that the average "hold" on video poker is about two percent higher than it would be if everyone played perfectly. Be thankful for those less skillful players who make it possible for the casinos to offer over 100% potential payback.

Chapter 6

I have encountered several unusual games in the ten years since I started playing video poker. Some would be very difficult to analyze due to their unique characteristics, and their apparent rarity would likely make it a wasted effort anyway, yet this book would be incomplete without at least some discussion of these games.

Some variations that appear at first glance to be short pay turn out to be even better in the long run than the standard full-pay machines, although they usually cause larger bankroll fluctuations. A few such variations are covered elsewhere in this book. Since strategy changes are required to take advantage of the variations, you should not attempt to play an unknown machine unless it's just for experimental reasons.

One-At-A-Time

By far the most uncommon game I have ever encountered was the One-At-A-Time. Basically a five-coin Draw Poker machine, it has five Instant Discard buttons instead of the usual Hold and Draw buttons. This game's payoff schedule starts with two pair or better, but you get an immediate replacement for each discard, one card at a time as the name says.

For example, suppose you are dealt J♥-9♥-3♣-7♥-8♥. You can try for a straight flush by discarding the 3♣, and the machine will even suggest that discard. If you catch the 10 of hearts, you would of course immediately press the Take button to claim the big payoff, but that's only one chance in 47. Now if you drew any heart or ten you would probably decide to Take the flush or straight payoff. Suppose, however, you catch the nine of spades. You can't discard that same card again, but you now have a pair of nines.

At this point you could discard the 9♥, hoping for any ten for the straight, but that's an inside draw, so you should discard the seven, eight or jack and try for another nine. If you discard the seven and catch a jack, you now have two pair, so you would discard the eight to try for a full house.

The game is over when all five cards have been replaced, when you press the Take button, or when it is no longer possible to achieve a payoff or to increase the payoff if you already have one. Confusing? That's the fun part; you have to stop and think ahead before making each discard, which makes this a game for those who enjoy puzzles.

Unfortunately these machines appeared in only a few casinos, and they didn't get much play, so we may never see them again. Perhaps the concept is too complicated for casual players. Perhaps they'll show up again somewhere.

I predict that innovations such as this will strongly supplement the proliferation of new games. This presents a problem, however, since such games are much harder to analyze than simple payoff schedule changes.

The Double Card

In the Double Card variation on Jacks-or-Better a 53rd card is added to the deck. No, it's not the joker, but it is a joke. If you have this "Double" card along with a high pair, two pair, trips or four-of-a-kind, you receive twice the normal payoff for that hand.

At first glance this looks great, but on closer inspection we find that it furtively *reduces* the payback. The added card will often get in the way of making a straight, flush, straight flush or royal. I have not bothered with a complete analysis on this game because there is about one percent net loss over the same payback schedule without the Double card.

For example, if you are dealt a four-card royal, you have one chance in 48 of catching the missing card for the jackpot, versus one in 47 on a standard Jacks-or-Better. There is a similar reduction in the chances of improving to a straight or flush. The net cost on any draw where the Double Card can't help is about two percent of that hand's expected value.

It even gets in the way with hands it *does* help. For example, in Jacks-or-Better the expected value of a pair of jacks with three irrelevant discards is 1.54. Drawing to a high pair and the Double Card, you might anticipate that the expected value would double to 3.08, but it increases only to 2.76. This is because of the reduced chances of making trips or quads, and a full house is impossible.

When dealt the Double Card, you should discard it unless you have a made pay that it works or when drawing to only one or two high cards or a small pair. Better yet, just avoid this game.

2nd Chance Progressives

The 2nd Chance machine is basically a flat top Jacks-or-Better, but it offers a one-card second draw if such a draw could improve the hand to a straight or better.

The second-chance payoffs are not the same as in the original pay-off schedule; instead they are determined according to the odds at the time. Although there are some cases where the second-chance draw offers 100% payback, it more often pays back less than 97%.

The notable exception is on a 2nd Chance progressive when the first draw results in four cards to a royal flush, in which case making a royal on the second chance pays the progressive jackpot. Since there is about one chance in 45 of hitting a royal in this situation, plus some more frequent small payoffs, this draw is well over 100% payback even at the progressive reset value of 250 coins.

A sizable jackpot can add one percent or more to the basic 99.5% payback, yielding well over 100% expectancy. If you are frustrated by all those four-card royals you've had then this may be the game for you.

However, unless the second chance jackpot is very large, be sure it's a full-pay (9/6) machine.

An interesting characteristic of these machines is that even if you play only one coin initially, you can still bet five coins on the 2nd Chance draw. The big surprise is that it can be more advantageous to play one coin instead of five until the opportunity arises to play for the progressive jackpot.

A more complete strategy for this very attractive game (sometimes as high as 106% payback) can be found in the November, 1994 issue of *Video Poker Times*.

Royal Court and Four-of-a-Kind Bonus Poker

The Royal Court is an 8/5 Jacks-or-Better with payoffs of 40-for-1 for four jacks, 60-for-1 for four queens, and 100-for-1 for four kings. The probability of any quads is .002363, and one in 12.08 of these will be jacks or higher (see "The Payoff Schedule —

Jacks-or-Better" on page 36) so the probability of any one of these particular quads is .002363 ÷ 12.08 = .000196 or almost .02%. Since these bonuses aren't big enough to trigger any changes in our Precision Play, we can add them up as follows:

Jacks: (40-25) x .0196 = +0.29%

Queens: (60-25) x .0196 = +0.69%

Kings: (100-25) x .0196 = +1.47%

Together, these bonuses add 2.45% to the 97.27% of the basic 8/5 machine, for a net long-term payback of 99.72%. But that's not the whole story. Some of these machines also offer $12,500 for a reversible royal, adding yet another .38%, bringing the total payback to 100.1%. If a basic 9/6 machine also pays $12,500 on the two-way sequential royal then its payback is about 99.88%. It's up to you to decide whether it's worth the larger bankroll fluctuations for the .22% gain.

The most common Four-of-a-Kind Bonus Poker is an 8/5 Jacks-or-Better paying 80-for-1 for quad aces and 40-for-1 for quad twos, threes, or fours, yielding a total payback of 99.16% Such machines might be considered marginally attractive when you are determined to play and there are no full-pay machines around, especially if your play can earn good comps.

There are too many variations of "bonus poker" to cover them all here but, since the strategy is generally unchanged, as long as the bottom end is basically an 8/5 Jacks-or-Better you can just add or subtract expected values to get the overall payback. For more specifics, see "The Benefit or Cost of Variations" on page 59.

Double Down Stud

The Double Down Stud machine looks something like a Jacks-or-Better, but it operates quite differently. The unique characteristic is that it deals only four cards, and you have the option of doubling your bet before the fifth card is dealt. There is no draw; any payoff is made as soon as the fifth card is shown.

Here's the payoff schedule:

Royal Flush *	2000
Straight flush	200
Four-of-a-kind	50
Full house	12
Flush	9
Straight	6
Three-of-a-kind	4
Two pair	3
Pair of jacks – aces	2
Pair of sixes – tens	1
* The royal pays only 1,000-for-1 if less than ten coins are bet.	

Double Down Stud requires almost no skill. With no discarding and only one card to come after the initial wager, the analysis is much simpler than for the other games. Obviously you should double if you have any pay made in the first four cards. Even if you have only a pair of sixes the worst you can do is break even. The only question, then, is: How good a hand do you need to double when no pay is made in four cards?

The obvious answer is to double whenever the expected value exceeds one. Let's look at a hand to see how this is done. Suppose we are dealt J-Q-4-4. There are 48 cards remaining unseen, of which there are three each jacks and queens to make two pair for an EV of (3+3)/48x3 = 18/48. There are also two more fours to make three-of-a-kind for an EV of 2/48x4 = 8/48. The total EV is only 26/48, which is less than one, so we don't double.

Double Down Stud Strategy
Double down if you have ...
Any made pay,
Any flush draw, or
Any open-ended straight draw.

A flush draw means that all four of the first four cards are the same suit. An open-ended straight draw means any four cards in sequence with no gap, 2-3-4-5 through 10-J-Q-K.

There are two types of zilch hands; those with a pair of deuces through fives, and those with no pair and no straight or flush possibilities. The baby pair hand might look good, but at only 26/48 payback as shown above, it's a big loser. The other zilch hands have an average EV of only 12/48.

The best zilch hand is A-K-Q-J (not all the same suit). There are twelve cards that will make a high pair (worth two), and four that will make a straight (worth six), for a total payback of 48. Doubling on a break-even bet merely increases your bankroll fluctuations (but a slot club rebate would make it a slightly positive play). Anything less than these four high cards will have a lower payback. Of course even the worst possible hand, 2-3-4-7 (not suited), could improve to a payoff by making a pair of sevens, but its EV is only 3/48.

My analysis of this game shows a long-term payback of 97.28%. Many people will double their bet on a baby pair, reducing the payback by yet another 3%.

With its low payback, it's not surprising that Double Down Stud has not become very popular. Most players pass them by or quit after only a short try. Even the 8/5 Jacks-or-Better machines are a better play at about the same payback.

The attractiveness has been improved some by adding a progressive jackpot on the royal, but since this is strictly a five-card game with no draw, the chance of a royal flush is only four in 2,598,960, or approximately one in 650,000. If you play 650 hands per hour, your can expect to average one royal per 1,000 hours of play, but this is in the long term. And what is the "long term" for this game? I have often suggested that the long term for games is enough play to expect at least five royals. Using that same criterion, the long term for Double Down Stud would be at least 5,000 hours of play. At 40 hours per week, that would be $2^1/_2$ years of full time play, so no one player will get anywhere near the "long term" before a large jackpot is hit.

Suppose the jackpot is at $45,000. Since we can expect one royal per 1,000 hours of play, does that make the game "worth" $45 per hour? Well, it does make the expected value of the jackpot worth

$45 per hour, but let's not overlook the expected losses along the way. The long-term payback of this game with a fixed jackpot is only 97.28%, and .3% of that is in the royal, resulting in an expected loss rate of little over 3% (about $35 per hour) while playing for the royal. Thus, the net expected value of the game is only about $10 per hour. The expected cost of a royal is about $35,000. Since this is a very low skill game, you have only the same chance of hitting it as any other player. To me, a game with such extreme volatility is not worth playing for $10 per hour.

Texas Hold'em

In a live hold'em game, you and up to ten other players each receive two cards, face down, and eventually there will be a total of five community cards in the middle of the table. Each player makes a poker hand using the best five out of the seven cards available to him (his two plus the community cards).

In the video version of Texas Hold'em, you deposit one coin, and the machine deals two cards to you and to each of four other "players." Only your two cards are exposed. You can fold immediately if it's a bad hand, or you can play a second coin to see the "flop" (the first three community cards). Again you can fold or play another coin to see the fourth card; and finally, you can play a fourth coin to see the last card.

If you play all four coins then the other players' hands are shown, and if you end up with the best hand you are paid according to the following schedule:

Royal flush	4000
Straight flush	250
Four-of-a-kind	75
Full house	30
Flush	25
Straight	18
Three-of-a-kind	14
One or two pairs	12
High card	10

Ties are "split" (you get one-half of the scheduled payoff, or one-third if two other players tie with you, and so on). In case of an odd unit the payoff is rounded down, so you would be paid only three coins for a three-way high card tie.

The other players' hands are also shown when you fold before the fourth coin, and you get your bet back if it turns out that your hand would have won (but not if it is tied). Since it always requires a four-coin bet to be able to win, a win with one or two pairs pays 3-for-1.

As with the One-At-A-Time machine, you have to make several decisions, and each decision is affected by new cards seen. It's difficult to ascertain the maximum long-term payback, but this game is interesting because of its similarity to a live hold'em game.

Unlike a live game, however, the other players never fold, so bluffing is not possible. Also, you can't check a mediocre hand; at each juncture you must either bet one coin or fold. Neither can you raise with a good hand, but the increased payoff for higher hands is somewhat analogous to a raise.

In any showdown type of game, the only correct strategy is to bet if the "pot odds" (the size of the pot divided by the bet) exceed your chance of winning. For example, if there is $20 in the pot and you must bet $2 to call, you are getting 10-to-1 (11-for-1) pot odds, so you should call if you estimate better than one chance in 11 of winning.

In this game, the "pot" is always the expected payoff, and the bet is always one more coin, so the pot odds are equal to the payoff. Therefore, you should bet another coin whenever the expected payoff exceeds the estimated odds against having the best hand.

Many people have attempted to analyze live hold'em by having a computer deal thousands of random combinations of community cards and opponents hands against each possible starting hand. (There are only 169 unique starting hands.) Poker experts deride this approach since it assumes that no one ever folds, but that is just the situation with this game so it may yield at least partially to such an analysis. So far, however, there has not been sufficient interest in this game to warrant the effort of developing a complete playing strategy.

Pick Five

Pick Five is the latest really new entrant on the video poker scene. After placing your bet, you are initially shown only two cards. You must select one of these two cards to become the first card of your final five-card hand. You are then shown two more cards, and again you pick one. This continues three more times, at which point your final five-card hand is complete. You are paid immediately if you have achieved a final hand that is in the payoff schedule.

Each time you are shown two cards, the card you don't pick is gone from the deck, so it will not appear again. This means that if you must pick from two cards of the same rank it will be impossible to make four-of-a-kind, and if you are shown two cards to a royal at the same time it will be impossible to make a royal.

The creator of this game tells me that an analysis on a supercomputer indicated a maximum payback of 103.1%, but so far no one has developed a strategy to achieve anywhere near that fantastic payback.

This is a very interesting game, but I predict that it will not be successful. My reasoning is similar to the One-At-A-Time; it is too complicated for recreational players, and the requirement to make five decisions instead of one makes it too slow to be attractive to the pros. If a strategy is developed to achieve a high expected hourly win rate, only the skilled players will give it extended play; the casinos will lose money on the game, and they will react by either removing the machines or reducing the payoff schedule, thus dooming it to limbo.

Actually, I hope my prediction is wrong, as I would like to see more interesting games (especially those with positive pay scales) proliferate.

MegaPoker

State-wide progressive jackpots, such as Megabucks and Quartermania reel slots, just had to come to video poker. The concept came first in the form of MegaPoker, but that game never achieved the popularity of its reel slot cousins. Its target market was limited to bars, restaurants, and small establishments; I've never seen it in a major casino. The bigger casinos seem to be more interested in their in-house progressives. Perhaps one reason is that MegaPoker has the same advantage over Megabucks as most video poker machines have over the reel slots; that is, you can determine the long-term payback by examining the payoff schedule. However, since some similar games may appear in the foreseeable future, it merits some attention here.

MegaPoker is basically a $1 8/5 Jacks-or-Better with a progressive jackpot that is paid only on a sequential royal flush in only one direction. The jackpot isn't likely to grow as large as other such progressives since it occurs somewhat more frequently. (OK, so it's only once in about 4,700,000 plays, but that's only medium term when compared to the Mega-type reel machines).

The statewide linkup of a large number of machines results in a rapidly growing jackpot, but can it compensate for the 8/5 payoff schedule? If the progressive jackpot were paid on any royal, Table 2 on page 160 tells us it need be only $2,330 x 4 = $9,320 for 100% payback. However, only one in 120 royals will be in the correct sequence, and the other 119 are paid only $4,000, so the jackpot would have to be about $640,000 for 100% total long-term payback — and that's not considering the income tax you would have to pay on such an amount. To net 100% after taxes, the jackpot would have to be about a million dollars. If it's paid over 20 years instead of immediately, it would have to be about $1.6 million. Such a large jackpot is extremely unlikely.

If you're in Las Vegas, the Fiesta offers full-pay 25¢ Jacks-or-Better that pays 60,000-for-5 for a royal that is in sequence in either direction. With no modifications to Precision Play, this game offers slightly over 100% payback, and the same modifications for sequential royal draws will increase that another .1%, so this machine is much more attractive.

On any machine with a large jackpot on a sequential royal, the three-card sequential royal moves up in value, and even a two-card sequential royal is sometimes worth drawing to. For example, if dealt 4♦-J♣-J♥-K♣-A♣ you would hold the J-K-A of clubs, whereas if the suited J-K-A were not in these exact positions (or the opposite) for a sequential royal, you would hold the pair of jacks. There are other strategy adjustments that can be made, but together they still have a minuscule affect on the overall payback.

If you're elsewhere in Nevada and are looking for a video poker with a big jackpot then MegaPoker may be tempting, but I can't recommend it if there are any full-pay machines available.

Five Deck Frenzy

Five Deck Frenzy is the latest entry into Mega-jackpot video poker. Instead of one deck of cards, this game is dealt from five 52-card decks. However, the decks are not all shuffled together; instead, each of the five card positions on the screen is dealt from its own deck, and each draw card also comes only from that position's deck.

As might be expected, the payoff schedule is much longer than for most video poker games. The progressive jackpot is paid for five aces of spades, which will occur only about once in 65,000,000 plays, which is much less frequently than a sequential royal on a single-deck game, so it grows much larger than MegaPoker's jackpot.

In spite of that, the game has not become very popular, probably because it is so different, the strategy is far from intuitive, and the payback has been estimated at only 98.8% with the progressive jackpot at $300,000. In addition, at least two casinos do not allow for the use of their slot club card with this game. Also, most serious video poker players are not particularly interested in super jackpots because of the inherently high volatility. (Five Deck Frenzy is covered in the July/August, 1998, issue of *Video Poker Times*.)

Five Deck Poker

This game is the same as Five Deck Frenzy except that the progressive jackpot for five aces of spades is gone and the payoff schedule has been enhanced for the flush and full house. The 10,000-coin top jackpot is paid on any identical five-of-a-kind. The total payback is a bit better than even the best payoff schedule for Five Deck Frenzy, and the volatility is lower. It's still under 100% payback, but it's a more interesting game.

Money Fever

Money Fever can be found on many Williams "Multi-Pay Plus" games. Basically a short-pay Jacks-or-Better, it goes into a bonus mode whenever you hit a flush, and for the next seven hands you receive a bonus for every card in your final hand that is the same suit as that flush. As you can imagine, the strategy gets weird when in the bonus mode. And again, it is recommended that you stick to the basic games that do not have a variety of exceptions to the rules. (Money Fever is covered in the May/June, 1998, issue of *Video Poker Times*.)

Pick Five Poker

This is a very different game in which you are offered a total of ten cards, but only two at a time. Of each two offered, you must pick one to become part of your final hand. The game has a theoretical maximum payback of 103.1%, but play is relatively slow (perhaps up to 400 hands per hour) due to the need to make five separate decisions for each hand. A detailed strategy that will yield over 102% payback is given in the November/December, 1998, issue of *Video Poker Times*. With that same strategy you will achieve very close to maximum payback if you can remember all cards not picked whose absence from the deck rules out certain final hands, and then skip those draws in the hand rank tables.

Pick'em Poker

In this game, which is found on many Bally *GameMaker* machines, you are initially dealt two cards that you must keep, then two more cards are displayed from which you must choose one to combine with those first two. This is your only decision. Two more cards are then dealt from the remaining deck to complete the hand, whereupon any payoff is made. Play is quite fast (perhaps up to 1000 hands per hour). The maximum payback is about 99.9%. Certain Midwest casinos make the game very attractive, however, with slot club rebates that may add up to 1.5%. The playing strategy is given in the January/February, 1999, issue of *Video Poker Times*.

Sneak Peek Poker

Sneak Peek is similar to regular Draw Poker, but before selecting the cards to hold you are given a "sneak peek" at the first card that you will receive on the draw. As of this writing, Sneak Peek is not offered with a payoff schedule that would put it over 100% payback. We haven't worked out a complete strategy for this game, but it is discussed briefly in the November/December, 1998, issue of *Video Poker Times*.

Big E Poker

Williams Gaming has introduced an entirely new concept to intrigue video poker players—a four hand poker game where you wager 10, 20, 30, 40 or 50 coins or credits. You get to place seventeen cards in an E-shaped pattern, and you are paid for all four hands. When you get one-third of the deck to play with, royal flushes, straight flushes, four of a kinds and full-houses abound. You can get a full-house (pays 40), a flush (pays 25), four of a kind (pays 100) and two pair (pays 10) and then collect the total of all the hands; that is, 175 credits. You are virtually certain of getting at least one paying hand. Big E is discussed in the July/August, 1999 issue of *Video Poker Times*.

What Does the Future Hold?

Video poker became the hottest innovation in gaming very quickly and, as noted before, new variations continue to appear with uncanny regularity. Most new games are not attractive because their maximum payback falls below 100%. Worse, a new type of variation has started to appear. Unlike the reel machines with total paybacks that are forever a mystery (except to the manufacturer and the casino), it is possible to calculate the payback of nearly all video poker machines because we know they deal randomly from a standard 52-card deck (or 53 cards with the joker). At least that's the case in Nevada where gaming regulators require and test for that randomness.

Some of the new games, however, add a special symbol such as a flag or star that may appear randomly on any card. The player receives a bonus if all cards of the hand have that symbol. We have no way to decide whether any strategy modifications are appropriate or to determine the maximum payback of these games since the machine does not disclose how frequently the special symbol will show up.

Another variation is a simulated reel slot that appears when you hit four of a kind, with no indication of the expected payoff (other than the maximum).

Such games are in a subclass somewhere between the regular video poker and the reel machines. If this trend continues, it may spell the end to video poker as we know it; it will no longer be the intelligent player's game. It depends on whether or not the general public flocks to the machines. If they ignore them the casino will remove them.

Video poker has grown at an amazing rate. As for blackjack, I believe that one important reason is the perception that the game can be beat, thus appealing to the player's ego and intelligence. Most players do not read the books, yet they do their own intuitive judgment which may often result in a higher payback than offered by the reel slots.

Why would the casinos want to undermine the player's main attraction to the game? The game manufacturers and casinos seem to be overlooking the fact that most video poker players moved over from the reel slots because the games are more interesting and because they have a payback and strategy which can be determined from the payoff schedule. Allow the perception that a game is beatable and you attract more players.

At least a few casino managers know that most players will never achieve the rated payback. This has been revealed in many promotions such as the Super-Full-Pay machines — full pay Jacks-or-Better with the flush or full house payoff *increased* by one, giving a 9/7 or 10/6 payoff schedule. Let's hope this becomes the dominant trend.

Chapter 7

Test Yourself

C lass is over. You've read the Precision Play strategies, but can you recall and apply the rules in an actual casino situation? What if you just bought this book and have only an hour or so to study before going to the casino? Worse, you don't have anyone to practice with. What should you do? A quick test of how much you've comprehended to this point should let you know quickly if you're ready to take the plunge. So, it's time to test yourself.

Before continuing, select only one type of machine. (Be sure it's a game that's available where you intend to play.) Study the Precision Play rules for that game only. After you're comfortable playing that game, you can branch out to others, but it will be nearly impossible to become a winning player if you try to tackle more than one variety at a time. If you're on a limited bankroll, I suggest starting with Jacks-or-Better. If you have a moderate bankroll, and you're in an area where there are some full pay Deuces Wild machines available, then I suggest starting with Deuces Wild.

The practice sessions are each divided into two parts — a series of predraw hands, and the correct play for each of those hands. You will gain the most from this if you don't look at the answers until after you've taken the entire quiz. Take a separate sheet of paper, write down the hand number, and note the cards to hold. For example, if the first hand looked like this:

1. Q♦ 4♠ 9♥ Q♠ 7♣

then you should answer: 1. Q♦ Q♠ (or Qd Qs).

After writing down all of your answers, check to see if you made any errors. In the strategies where the rules are numbered, the circled number after the answer refers to the pertinent Precision Play rule. Be sure you understand the reason for each decision before you continue because this will increase the speed of your reactions.

If you don't understand the reason for a rule, or if you think there is an error in the answer, refer to the respective Table 2, 3 or 4 in Appendix B on page 157. In every case you should be holding the cards with the highest expected value (highest position in the table).

Now of course I could make an error and give a wrong answer. Some authors might even put in a wrong answer on purpose to make you think. I did not do that, however, so if you find you disagree with any answer given, please write to me (either snailmail or e-mail) and explain your reasoning.

These quizzes don't cover all of the possibilities, but your score will give a good indication of how well you know the rules. If you miss more than one it would be a good idea to study some more before risking your money in the casino.

Following these quizzes is a discussion on practicing at home. Take whatever time is necessary to become at least 90% accurate before playing, and then continue to improve your play as you go. If you think you don't have the time to practice because you want to get to the casino and play, consider what your playing errors might cost. Wouldn't it be even more fun playing the machines if you have a genuine chance of beating them?

Okay, you've selected one of the basic machine types, and you've pretty much committed the Precision Play rules to memory. Go ahead to the Practice Session that's specific to that game. Don't try to take the quiz on other types; you will only confuse yourself with the cases where the play is different for the same starting hand (e.g., as when you're dealt two pair or an inside straight draw).

The Jacks-or-Better quiz follows. If you selected Deuces Wild or Joker Wild, skip now to the respective Practice Session. Do not take the quiz for more than one game type at a time.

Practice Session: Jacks-or-Better

Read the "Final Exams" section (preceding) and study the Precision Play rules for Jacks-or-Better before taking this quiz. For the best results, select the cards to hold in all pre-draw hands shown before looking at any of the answers.

Use a separate sheet of paper to write down the cards to hold for each of these dealt hands:

1.	4♦	J♥	3♦	A♦	J♦
2.	10♦	8♠	J♥	9♦	J♦
3.	7♦	8♥	3♦	A♦	8♠
4.	7♦	8♥	3♦	A♦	8♦
5.	5♣	7♥	5♦	5♠	5♥
6.	K♣	J♣	9♣	6♣	Q♣
7.	K♣	J♣	9♣	6♥	Q♣
8.	K♣	J♣	A♣	6♣	Q♣
9.	J♣	9♣	10♥	Q♣	6♣
10.	K♣	10♠	10♥	Q♦	J♠
11.	9♣	10♠	10♥	Q♦	J♠
12.	3♦	9♣	2♠	5♦	A♦
13.	3♦	A♣	2♦	5♦	A♦
14.	3♦	9♣	2♠	4♥	A♦
15.	Q♠	A♣	J♠	7♣	K♥
16.	Q♦	A♠	J♠	7♣	K♥
17.	Q♦	A♠	J♠	7♣	3♥
18.	Q♦	A♥	J♠	7♣	3♥
19.	3♥	9♦	K♥	10♥	6♠
20.	3♣	J♦	Q♥	10♥	6♠

Following are the correct answers for the preceding Jacks-or-Better hands. The circled number references the pertinent Precision Play rule. For example, ② refers to rule No. 2. In a few cases, more than one rule is referenced. You may want to refer to Table 2 on page 160 occasionally if clarification is needed.

1. J♥ J♦   ②   You didn't hold the ace, did you? Two pair pays the same no matter what the rank of the second pair, and holding a kicker reduces the chances of catching another jack. Also, we don't break the made pay for a flush draw. If we were playing in a tournament, however, we would probably go with the double inside straight flush draw (A-3-4 of diamonds).

2. J♥ J♦   ②   Don't break a high pair even for the open-ended straight or straight flush three-draw.

3. 8♥ 8♣   ③   There is no reason to break this pair, but...

4. 7♦ 3♦ A♦ 8♦   ③   ...we do break a low pair to draw only one card to a flush.

5. 5♣ 7♥ 5♦ 5♠ 5♥   That's right, *hold all five cards*. Quads can't be improved in this game, so let's minimize the chance of inadvertently dropping a card.

6. K♣ J♣ 9♣ 6♣ Q♣   ①   The pat flush *is* better than two pair. Don't break it for only a three-card royal or an inside straight flush draw. (But for tournament play we would probably break the flush and go for the royal.)

7. K♣ J♣ 9♣ Q♣   There is no rule that says to break a four-card straight flush (even an inside draw such as this) for a three-card royal, so we hang on to the nine.

8. K♣ J♣ A♣ Q♣   ①   Break the pat flush for a four-card royal. Similarly, we would break a high pair, or we would break a straight by discarding an off-suit ten.

9.   J♣ 9♣ Q♣ 6♣   ⑤   The flush draw is obviously much better than the straight draw.

10. K♣ 10♠ Q♦ J♣   ③   It's worth breaking the low pair (tens) for an open end straight draw with three high cards.

11. 10♠ 10♥   ③   There is nothing worth breaking the pair.

12. 3♦ 5♦ A♦   ⑥   These low straight flush draws are often overlooked.

13. 3♦ 2♦ 5♦ A♦   ②⑥   No comment needed.

14. A♦   ⑨   You didn't seriously consider the inside straight draw, did you?

15. Q♠ J♠   ⑦   No comment needed.

16. Q♦ A♠ J♠ K♥   ⑦   No comment needed.

17. A♠ J♠   ⑧⑨   No comment needed.

18. Q♦ J♠   ⑨   No comment needed.

19. K♥   ⑩   We don't hold the ten because one of the discards is the same suit. However, this is a very close decision, and the loss would not be significant if we always held a suited ten with a king when there is no better draw.

20. J♦ Q♥   ⑩   Two high cards are almost always better than one high card with a suited 10.

Practice Session: Deuces Wild

Read the "Final Exams" section and study the Precision Play rules for Deuces Wild before taking this quiz. For the best results, select the cards to hold in all predraw hands shown before looking at any of the answers. To get a better understanding, you may want to refer occasionally to Table 3 on page 162. You will notice many cases where the play is completely different from what it would be when dealt the same hand in Jacks-or-Better. That is why I recommend learning one game thoroughly before trying a second type of machine.

Use a separate sheet of paper to write down the cards to hold for each of these dealt hands:

1.	8♦	J♥	A♥	8♠	J♦
2.	10♦	J♥	3♦	A♦	J♦
3.	7♦	8♦	3♦	A♦	8♣
4.	7♦	8♥	3♦	A♦	9♣
5.	9♣	K♥	9♦	9♠	9♥
6.	K♣	J♣	9♣	10♣	Q♣
7.	K♣	J♣	9♣	6♥	Q♣
8.	K♣	J♣	A♣	2♦	Q♣
9.	J♣	9♣	K♥	7♣	8♠
10.	K♠	2♥	10♠	10♥	Q♠
11.	9♣	10♠	10♣	J♣	5♣
12.	3♦	9♣	2♠	5♦	A♥
13.	3♥	9♣	2♦	8♣	2♠
14.	3♣	9♣	2♦	8♣	2♠
15.	Q♠	A♣	J♥	2♣	2♥
16.	Q♦	A♦	Q♠	2♣	2♥
17.	2♦	A♠	J♠	2♣	2♥
18.	2♦	A♥	2♠	2♣	2♥
19.	2♥	10♦	10♥	2♠	2♣
20.	2♥	9♦	9♥	2♠	2♣
21.	Q♠	K♥	7♥	10♠	3♠
22.	K♠	J♠	8♦	5♠	3♣

The rules for Deuces Wild aren't numbered, but you can find the appropriate rule by looking under the number of deuces in the hand. Following are the correct plays for the Deuces Wild practice hands.

1. Hold either pair, but not both. This is just one of the many differences between Jacks-or-Better and Deuces Wild.

2. In this game the three-card royal is better than the pair. Another difference between Jacks-or-Better and Deuces Wild.

3. The pair is better than the four-card flush draw. Yet another difference.

4. There is nothing here worth holding. Just draw five new cards. High cards have no particular value in this game.

5. Hold just the four nines. Unlike Jacks-or-Better, the wild cards make it possible to improve to five-of-a-kind.

6. Break the straight flush! Discard the nine and go for the royal. Unlike Jacks-or-Better, the straight flush isn't a high paying hand.

7. Draw for the straight flush.

8. Hold the wild royal. It's worth much more than the four-card natural royal draw. However, if the royal flush is worth at least 1,080 bets ($1,350 on a five-coin quarter machine), it becomes correct to drop the deuce and go for the natural royal. This could happen on a machine with a progressive jackpot or if you have a bonus coupon.

9. Hold the three-card straight flush. Although the inside straight draw has the same expected value in this particular case, that would not be true if the straight card that was not part of the straight flush draw was outside the straight flush.

10. Break the three-of-a-kind for the four-card wild royal draw. (That is, hold everything except the ten of hearts).

11. The pair is better than either the three-card straight flush or the four-card flush draw.

12. Draw four cards to the deuce. (You weren't tempted to hold that ace with the deuce, were you?)

13. Hold the eight and nine of clubs with the deuces.

14. Same as #13. Remember that the flush pays only 2-for-1. The suited discard reduces the expected value slightly, but not enough to change the strategy.

15. Draw to the deuces alone. With two deuces we're not impressed with any made pay less than quads.

16. Hold the made quads in preference to the wild royal draw. Discard only the ace.

17. Hold the wild royal. Yes, it's tempting to draw for the four deuces, but it's a money-losing play. The wild royal is worth 25-for-1 while the draw to the three deuces has an expected value slightly less than 15.

18. Hold all five cards. Four deuces can't be improved, so let's minimize the possibility of inadvertently dropping a card.

19. Hold the five-of-a-kind. Discarding the tens reduces the chances of a wild royal.

20. There's a tiny gain in expected value by breaking the low five-of-a-kind to draw to the three deuces. However, many pros will always hold the five-of-a-kind, feeling that the time required for the 1,000-coin payoff and a likely need for a fill (or for a hand pay) more than offsets the slight gain in EV.

21. Hold the suited Q-10.

22. Draw five cards. The suited K-J is not a good draw because of the suited discard. In fact you wouldn't lose much by never drawing to a king-high two-card royal.

Practice Session: Joker Wild

Read the "Final Exams" section and study the Precision Play rules for Joker Wild before taking this quiz. For the best results, select the cards to hold in all predraw hands shown before looking at any of the answers. To get a better understanding, you may want to refer occasionally to Table 4 on page 164.

Use a separate sheet of paper to write down the cards to hold for each of these dealt hands (JR stands for joker).

1.	9♣	10♦	9♦	JR	K♦
2.	4♦	4♥	JR	5♦	7♦
3.	4♦	4♥	JR	5♦	8♦
4.	7♦	8♥	3♦	9♦	6♠
5.	K♣	K♥	A♣	5♠	10♣
6.	K♣	J♣	9♣	10♣	Q♣
7.	4♦	J♣	9♣	8♥	10♣
8.	K♣	J♣	A♣	JR	Q♣
9.	J♣	9♣	10♥	Q♣	8♣
10.	9♣	7♣	7♥	8♣	3♣
11.	K♣	7♣	7♥	Q♣	J♣
12.	3♦	9♣	2♠	5♦	A♦
13.	4♦	Q♦	JR	5♦	3♦
14.	4♦	Q♦	JR	5♦	7♦
15.	2♣	Q♠	JR	5♦	7♠
16.	3♠	2♠	5♠	JR	K♥
17.	3♠	7♠	4♠	JR	A♥
18.	3♠	A♠	4♠	JR	A♥
19.	3♥	9♦	K♥	J♥	6♠
20.	3♥	JR	A♥	Q♥	6♠
21.	Q♣	5♥	7♣	9♥	10♣
22.	Q♣	J♥	7♣	9♥	10♣

As in the Jacks-or-Better practice session, the circled number references the pertinent rule, but here we have two sets of rules depending on whether the hand includes the joker. Therefore, X② refers to rule No. 2 *without* the Joker, and J② refers to rule No. 2 *with* the Joker.

Following are the correct plays for the Joker Wild practice hands.

1. 10♦ 9♦ **JR** K♦   J③   This three-card double-inside straight flush *does* include a king.

2. 4♦ **JR** 5♦ 7♦   J③   The single-inside straight flush draw doesn't require a king or ace.

3. 4♦ 4♥ **JR**   J③   There is no reason to break the trips.

4. 7♦ 8♥ 9♦ 6♠   X⑤   No comment necessary.

5. K♣ A♣ 10♣   X②   No comment necessary.

6. K♣ J♣ 9♣ 10♣ Q♣   X①   No comment necessary.

7. J♣ 9♣ 8♥ 10♣   X⑤   The four-card straight draw takes precedence over the three-card straight flush draw.

8. K♣ J♣ A♣ **JR** Q♣   J①   You wouldn't break a wild royal, would you?

9. J♣ 9♣ Q♣ 8♣   X①   No comment necessary.

10. 9♣ 7♣ 8♣ 3♣   X③   There is no rule saying you should break the four-card flush.

11. K♣ Q♣ J♣   X②   The three-card royal *is* better than a four-card flush.

12. 3♦ 5♦ A♦   X⑤   Any straight flush draw is better than just an ace.

13. 4♦ **JR** 5♦ 3♦   J②   No comment necessary.

14. 4♦ Q♦ **JR** 5♦ 7♦   J②   This straight flush draw is *not* open-ended, so hold the flush.

15. **JR** 5♦   J⑥   Holding one midcard with the joker is an often missed play. The seven would be just as good as the five.

16. 3♠ 2♠ 5♠ **JR**   J④   No comment necessary.

17. 3♠ 7♠ 4♠ **JR**   J④   The double inside straight flush draw is much better than the high pair.

18. A♠ **JR** A♥	J① No comment necessary.
19. K♥ J♥	X⑦ No comment necessary.
20. **JR** A♥	X⑧ Holding the ace alone with the joker is better than also holding the suited honor (the queen) with it due to the suited discard (the three of hearts).
21. Q♣ 10♣	X⑩ No comment necessary.
22. Q♣ J♥ 9♥ 10♣	X⑤ The straight draw is better than the two card royal.

Practicing Video Poker At Home

If you are planning a trip, and you want to be prepared to play video poker without having to constantly refer to this book, you can practice at home. If you have a computer, the best way to practice is with one of the video poker games. There are several good programs available for $30 or less, such as *Video Poker Tutor*, that are designed especially for this purpose. For a review of several such programs, see issue 3.2 of *Video Poker Times*.

If you don't have a computer, you can find hand-held electronic video poker games in the gift shops, gaming stores, by mail order, and often even in department or discount stores for about $10 to $150. Most of these keep track of credits, making it easy to practice your Precision Play while they keep track of your wins and losses. The LCD display is not nearly as pleasant to look at as the color screen on the real machines or on a computer, but it's adequate for practice. Some of these machines allow two players to alternate play, and they keep a separate record of each player's credits. (Most of those I've seen are made in China, so follow your own conscience in purchasing something that may have been produced with slave labor.) Of course you can buy a real (used) "made in USA" video poker machine for about $995 and up, but check your local laws first: It's a criminal offense to own "gaming devices" in some states. The shortcoming with any of these machines is that they don't tell you when you make a bad play as the computer program will.

If you don't have a computer or one of these other machines, you can still have a practice session. Just take out a standard deck of playing cards, several rolls of coins (or poker chips, or any other convenient tokens or markers), and sit down at the kitchen table.

For simplicity, each token will represent one bet (five coins) since we will nearly always bet the maximum number of coins on a real machine. You can do it alone if necessary, but this works best with two people. Here's how it works.

"P" will be the player, and "M" will act as the machine. P starts with a known number of tokens.

To start each game, P gives M one token. M shuffles the deck and deals five cards face up in a row.

P may refer to the Precision Play strategy rules if necessary, then select which cards to hold and discard the remaining upcards. M then deals the top cards off the deck to replace the discards. If the final hand is worth a pay, M pays P the appropriate number of tokens.

To start out, you should keep the payoff table and strategy rules handy for the game being practiced, but you'll soon have them both memorized without really trying. After some practice, P should try to make decisions without referring to the rules, and M should check P's decisions against the strategy and inform P of any errors.

You may want to keep track of payoffs on paper rather than handling so many tokens, just as the more convenient machines keep track of credits rather than requiring you to insert five coins for each play. Even better, use a pocket calculator to keep track of credits. Of course, you can practice without tracking wins and losses, but the record helps to acquaint you with the fluctuations you can expect in your bankroll. After a while the two players should switch roles so that each gets some practice.

Another alternative is for two or more people to query each other about the rules or to use a deck of cards to set up hands that exhibit some of the closer decisions. But however you do it, be prepared *before* risking your money in the casino.

Chapter 8

The Value of Slot Clubs and Comps

Believe it or not, at one time casinos completely ignored slot players. They issued "comps" (complimentary hotel rooms, meals, drinks, etc.) freely to players in the pit, but almost never to slot players. Today, however, casinos realize so much revenue from slots that they actually court players. One of the ways they do this is through comps. This is good news for the video poker player because comps increase a game's overall payback as well as your enjoyment. You can increase your edge by joining every slot club you can find and accepting the free drinks, plus the bonuses that some casinos add to a jackpot.

Slot clubs typically return around .05% to .5% of your total wagers, but at least three casinos offer up to .67% in cash (plus comps), and at least two pay 1% or more on reel slots, adding this amount to your payback. Any of these may occasionally be increased by double or triple points promotions. For the best information on slot clubs, I recommend Jeffrey Compton's *Guide to Slot Clubs* (see Appendix F on page 186).

If you think that it's not worthwhile joining some slot clubs because their rebate values are so small, think again. When I first started playing, I passed up some slot clubs because the rebate was less than one tenth of one percent and the rewards came in food comps only. Then a friend showed me the coupons he had received in the mail shortly after joining one of those clubs and playing only a couple rolls of quarters. His mailer included: an ace for the first card in blackjack for up to a $10 bet; three $5 match plays, food "twofers" and a coupon for a weekend stay at less than half the regular room rate. After that, I made it a point to join the slot club at every casino I visit and play at least a couple rolls of quarters even if the best game offered is ordinary Jacks-or-Better.

As far as most local players are concerned the best slot clubs pay a cash rebate, but of course they're not very interested in the discounted room rates. If you're from out of town, then room comps can be very valuable to you. Select whatever type of benefits are

105

most important to you, but don't let the slot club alone determine where you play. It's usually much more important that they have high paying games of the kind you like.

Casinos advertise their slot clubs in various ways, each trying to make it sound as if theirs is the best with ads such as "Our points are worth twice as much." Twice as much as what? They don't say. Neither do they say how much action it takes for each point, so you'll probably have to figure it out for yourself. Here's how.

First, you need to know how much play the casino requires for each point and how many points you have to earn for each dollar rebate. In some cases, this information is given in the club's brochure. If not, you'll have to ask, but a few casinos still have what Jeffrey Compton calls a "Don't ask, won't tell" policy. In such a case, your only reliable source of information may be the experience of a knowledgeable player.

Many casinos now make it simple by giving one point for each dollar of action (e.g., four plays on a five-coin quarter machine will yield five points). If it then requires 500 points for a $1 cash back, then the rebate is $1 ÷ $500.00 x 100% = 0.2%. For others the arithmetic is not so simple, but the method is the same. Suppose 15 quarters generates one point, and 2,000 points yields a buffet comp that would cost $8.95 plus tax ($9.58 total). In this case, it takes 15 x 25¢ = $3.75 of action to get one point, and it takes 2,000 ÷ $9.58 = 209 points for each dollar of comp value. Thus $3.75 x 209 = $783 of action yields $1 comp value back, so the rebate is $1.00 ÷ $783 x 100% = 0.128% or roughly one-eighth of one percent.

There are other things that can add to your payback and enjoyment. A drink would typically cost between $1 and $3, but most casinos comp drinks for players, and most will comp any brand they have at the bar. Do you have a taste for Courvoisier or Chevis Regal? If you enjoy one "free" drink worth $2 every 300 plays at $1.25 per play, that's equivalent to adding .53% to the game's payback. Of course you usually tip the server, but you would probably tip the same if you paid for the drink. No matter how much you might enjoy that touch of alcohol, it's really best to choose coffee, juices or soft drinks so you don't dull your senses and make playing errors — at least until you're about ready to quit for the day (but please don't drink and drive).

Some casinos offer other bonuses. For example, the Plaza in downtown Las Vegas currently mails players a coupon good for a free dinner for two with any slot or video poker payoff of $200 or more (as with many promotions, you must call a slot attendant while the payoff is still on the screen). The menu prices on the dinners range from $6.95 to $9.95, so the coupon is worth about $15 to $21. Suppose you value this coupon at $20. If you're playing quarter Deuces Wild, four deuces pays the equivalent of $270 instead of $250, thus adding about .08% to the total payback. Many casinos offer such perks, so be sure to check out the signs, and ask if you're not sure. And when you do your research, be sure to ask if you have to call a slot attendant to verify your win and give you your coupon. At least one Las Vegas casino reprogrammed their slot club computers to automatically credit an account when they qualified for a special promotion. This move not only saves wear and tear on change personnel, it also saves you valuable playing minutes. However, this is not a common practice, so be aware that you usually have to stop playing until your qualifying payoff is verified.

It's also a good idea to watch for seasonal bonuses. Many casinos give free candy with any payoff of $5 or more on holidays such as Mother's Day and Valentine's Day. On a quarter Deuces Wild, that's any four-of-a-kind or better, or about one every 14 plays! Some people go home with a whole case of candy. I suspect that much of it goes to waste unless they give it away — which again saves gift-buying money — but I have seen some people eat it as fast as they get it.

But there are more significant seasonal promotions, especially during slow times of the year in Las Vegas such as the hottest part of summer and between Thanksgiving and Christmas. You'll find double and triple points, but it's things like double on certain four-of-a-kinds or even on a royal flush that are more interesting to serious players.

Slot clubs and their accompanying bonuses are very important to players. And, perhaps nobody has more insight into this special than Jeffrey Compton. For that reason, the following is excerpted from the "Slot Club News" column in the September/October, 1996 issue of *Video Poker Times*. In that column, Jeffrey Compton said:

"In my book, *Guide to Slot Clubs,* I differentiate between tangible and intangible slot club benefits. Tangibles are advertised by the casino. For example, the Mirage gives .67% cash back on total coin-in. The Fiesta gives one point for every dollar played, and 2,500 points will get you a Sunday Brunch. Once you have completed the required play, you can collect (or consume) the benefits any time up to one year after your last play. Though casinos can change their point structure and benefit schedule, it requires considerable reprinting and retraining expenditures, not to mention goodwill losses.

"Intangibles are unadvertised additional perks. At the Mirage, about 200 points ($3,000 coin-in) will get you a buffet for two in addition to your cash back. At Sam's Town, 3,000 points (also equal to $3,000 coin-in) is usually good for dinner for two at Papamio's. You've noticed that I use the terms "about" and "usually" in this paragraph. With intangible benefits, there is nothing on paper so it is totally up to the casino management.

"Several criteria come into play including day of the week, time of the year, what game you play, how well you play and how recently you played. At Circus Circus properties, additional comps must be used within 72 hours of play. Sam's Town seems to allow two weeks. The Golden Nugget gives you 72 hours from the time you redeem your points for cash. Several Reno casinos insist that you consume all benefits within 24 hours of play. And again, this could change tomorrow via a management memo.

"So what is your best defense? The most effective and easiest strategy is to develop a relationship with the casino hosts. They can tell you about any special policies or rules and, in many cases, can stretch those rules to accommodate you.

"Another tactic is to open a credit line. Management is nicer to established customers with known finances. Recently several casinos, including Fitzgerald's, Treasure Island and Boomtown [now Silverton], mailed credit applications to their slot club members. When I returned a completed application to Boomtown, I was given a coupon good for complimentary dinner for two.

"And finally, if possible, learn to exaggerate your losses to the casino. A common trick is to pull your slot club card from the reader when you get four-of-a-kind or better. This prevents the win from being completely tallied on the slot club computer. An IGT man recently told me to also remove my slot club card before I cash out the machine. (Do not do this at The Orleans, Gold Coast or Barbary Coast as it will significantly affect your point balance.) Effective slot card pullers can decrease their gross win by five to seven percent and look like big losers. Casinos like losers."

Why do Casinos Have Slot Clubs?

There are many reasons why casinos have slot clubs, and each slot department manager or promotions manager probably has different reasons. Some possibilities include:

- Once you join their club, you may be likely to play there more often than in other casinos.

- Identification is required, so they will have you on their mailing list for future promotions. (Mailing lists are valuable and may be sold, but that's not likely because most casinos are probably jealous of their customer lists.)

- The casino's computer will record when and how much you play. Most clubs now record all of your wins and losses, and some will give you a printed summary at the end of the year on request. (How long will it be before the IRS demands this data?)

Some casinos have made a big thing of *not* having a slot club, claiming that it allowed them to pay more jackpots or to set the machines for higher payback. These claims may or may not be true with reel slots since it's impossible for us to determine the actual payback. Assuming they are not biased, however, we can determine the payback of most video poker games just by analyzing the payoff schedule, so the payback of the machine itself is not affected by the presence or absence of a slot club.

It's interesting to note that during such ads in Las Vegas several years ago, one casino that has a good slot club (.25% cash rebate) also had many full-pay machines, some with 4700-coin jackpots. Another that touted the absence of a slot club had only 4,000-coin jackpots and very few full-pay machines (but it did offer good food comps).

The moral is to consider all factors when selecting a casino and a game. Don't depend on the advertising but on what you see. A cash payback slot club will often compensate for the difference between a 4700-coin and a 4,000-coin jackpot, but it seldom comes close to making up for short pays on a full house (Jacks-or-Better and Double Bonus Poker) or on quads (Deuces Wild and Joker Wild).

When shopping around, look first for full-pay machines and meaningful bonus payouts. Then, if the casino has games you like, check out other factors such as slot clubs and comps. In some cases, however, a poorly thought out promotion may add enough side benefits to make almost any game attractive (see next section).

Promotions

From time to time casinos offer promotions in an attempt to attract new regular customers and increase their profits. Some are short-lived, and some last a long time. The temporary promotions rarely seem to actually benefit the casino to any great extent, but the ones that are connected to their video poker games are often a great boon to a skilled player who can analyze their value.

Perhaps the all-time best video poker promotion (or the worst from the casino's viewpoint) was held by a Las Vegas area casino during the first year it opened. For two days, they paid an additional 125 coins on all natural quads. This increased the payback on most games to over 104%, and every knowledgeable player from miles around was there day and night. The casino paid out millions extra in two days and even ran out of cash the second evening, but when the promotion ended almost everybody left, and the place was just as deserted as before. The casino had given away a lot of money, but instead of attracting new players, the promotion had an adverse effect in that the regulars were frustrated by not being able to get on their favorite machines and went elsewhere.

Several months later this same casino sent letters to slot club members offering a $20 for $10 coin buy-in. The problem was that you had to take the letter to the promotions booth on a certain day to have it validated. I went there to claim the free $10, but the line was very long. I asked someone at the front of the line how long they had been waiting, and she said over half an hour. Not wanting to stand in line that long, even for a free $10, I decided to have dinner first.

An hour later, the line was still just as long, so I left without playing. Why can't casino managers grasp the concept that a promotion should be designed to attract new players and convert them to regulars instead of frustrating customers that may already be regulars? Many of those people were so tired after waiting in line that they just got the extra $10, cashed out, and left.

They next mailed out coupons that could be used at the main cashier. This saved a little time, but the lines were still long. Why not coupons that could be used directly with a coin purchase from any change person? Think how much better off the casino would be if all those people were playing instead of standing in line. And, think about how cost-effective it would become by eliminating the need for additional personnel.

In creating promotions or installing high-payback machines, the maximum benefit to the casino seems to be achieved when the games (including promotions) return between 101% and 101.5% with optimum play (on quarter machines). If the payback is higher than this, and the casino has not had the foresight to provide an abundance of the desirable machines, they will be quickly saturated by pros.

One very common and effective promotion is to award drawing tickets for each payout above a certain level (most commonly 100 coins or any quads). Drawings are held at regular intervals, and winners must be present to collect. This is very effective at bringing in customers and keeping them there. As a player, you should plan to play all day at a given casino offering this type of promotion in order to derive the maximum return from it.

Another type of promotion is to double or triple the slot club points awarded for each dollar played for a limited period. This does bring people into the casino, but most of them were already customers (else how would they have a slot club card?), and few of them that wouldn't have been there anyway remain after the promotion ends.

One problem from the player's point of view is that if a casino already offers many high-payback machines, a promotion on top of that will make the machines so attractive to pros that they are overplayed and often taken out. Thus both the casino and its regular customers ultimately lose.

Many players regularly supplement their income just playing games with a positive expectancy, such as Deuces Wild, while others work the progressives or take advantage of good situations created by unsuspecting recreational players. Of course these players also take advantage of free food, discounted room rates, and other benefits of the slot clubs. However, there is more to be made by taking advantage of the many promotions offered to entice players into the casinos. In fact, many pros depend upon the promotions for a significant part of their income.

Obviously you will get the most out of video poker if you are able to take advantage of many worthwhile promotions, but to do that you must be able to evaluate a promotion for yourself. I'll give a few examples here to get you started, but casinos are very inventive at coming up with new ways to attract players. Fortunately for us, many of those promotion managers are not very good mathematicians, so they sometimes "give away the store." If you can outthink the casino, you can reap your fortune.

There are at least six ways to learn about promotions. In order of increasing importance, they are:

1. **Visit the casinos.** Sometimes when you enter a casino you will see a sign announcing a promotion. Or there may be brochures at the slot club booth or cage. This is not a very reliable way to learn about promotions since you would have to visit a lot of casinos every day.

2. **Newsletters.** You will get a lot of valuable information from a good newsletter, but unfortunately this is not the best place to learn about promotions, primarily because newsletters are not published frequently enough to tell you about short-lived promotions.

3. **Web sites.** There are numerous web sites that provide information about gambling opportunities. As might be expected, news of the best opportunities may be sold to subscribers rather than being reported to the general public, but you sometimes get some very useful information. A quick search for "video poker" with one of the more popular search engines will get you started.

4. **Ads.** Unlike the above which often provide information only after the promotion has begun, the casinos themselves often provide advance notice of good opportunities. The local newspapers are the best, followed by the free papers and the tourist magazines. Making use of this information, however, requires that you are able to evaluate promotions for yourself.

5. **Slot clubs.** Again, it is the casinos that provide advance notice of opportunities. In fact, some of the promotions are made available only to slot club members, and the mailings often include coupons not available to non-members. Thus you should join every slot club around to get on their mailing lists.

6. **Pro networks.** If you aspire to be a pro, you must get in contact with other pros and share information with them. If you see a very serious player, especially one playing two machines, try to start a conversation; you may make contact with a pro. See the section "The Professional Video Poker Player" for more information.

Now let's take a look at some promotions and see how to evaluate them.

One of the most common promotions is a bonus on four-of-a-kind (quads). How much would be added to a regular Jacks-or-Better game if a casino offers to pay an additional 100 coins on any quads? "The Payoff Schedule — Jacks-or-Better" shows that the regular 125-coin payoff for quads yields 5.91% of the payback. With no strategy changes, adding 100 coins to the payoff would add 100/125 of 5.91%, or 4.73%, bringing the total payback to 104.25%. Perhaps more significantly, even the short-term payback (excluding the royal and straight flush) becomes 101.7%. If you normally play 600 hands per hour then you probably net about 500 after waiting for the hand pay of the extra coins, so your total action is about 500 x $1.25 = $625 per hour. Your short-term expected gain is 1.7% of that or .017 x $625 = $10.60 per hour, and your long-term expectancy is 4.73% of that or nearly $30 per hour! (Although this bonus is not enough of a change to affect the playing strategy, adjustments are sometimes necessary to best take advantage of some payoff changes. Such adjustments would obviously change the final hand frequencies and hence the payback calculations. In such a case, these simple calculations would indicate the *minimum* increase in payback.)

And that's just on quarter machines. What if this same promotion applies to the $5 machines? All else being equal, you would have a short term expected win rate of over $200 per hour and a long term rate of nearly $600 per hour.

Another type of promotion is a bonus on a royal flush. A typical such bonus is an extra $199 on a quarter machine, bringing it to

$1,199, just $1 short of the threshold for a W-2G report. This would trigger a few small strategy changes, but the payback increase is quite small so we won't go into details here.

This time, let's play Deuces Wild.

"The Payoff Schedule — Deuces Wild" shows that 1.77% of the payback comes from the royal. The bonus adds 199/1,000 of that or about .35%. Adding this to the game's 100.75% basic payback gives a total payback of 101.1%. As you can see, this is not nearly as valuable as the quads bonus, and it's also a long term as opposed to a short-term increase, but such a bonus is often the best available at the time.

Tournament Play

There are lots of slot tournaments and blackjack tournaments, and more recently video poker tournaments have become more frequent. There are two basic types of tournaments — those with a buy-in, which might be anywhere from $25 to several hundred dollars, and those with free entry.

For a "free" tournament, the casino puts up the prize money, so your potential loss is no more than the time involved while your potential win is the top prize. These promotions are not generally open to just anyone who wants to enter. They usually are part of a promotion package, such as a room and show, or to slot club members by invitation, so if you like tournaments this is one more reason to join every slot club you see. Occasionally, however, the free tournament will be just that — free. However, you may have to play elimination levels that require you (should you qualify) to remain in the casino for the remaining levels.

A buy-in tournament may be open to anyone who is willing to pay the entry fee. Typically all of the buy-in money goes into the prize pool, but the casino may take a small percentage for running the tournament so it's best to ask first. If all of the fees go into the prize pool then it's a 100% expectation situation; if they take out a percentage, then the average player's expectation is reduced by that amount. In some cases, there might be a guaranteed prize; this may be dependent upon getting enough entrants, but I have heard of cases where the casino put up the difference when there were too few entrants, making the player's expectation over 100%.

The tournament is usually played on some standard game such as Jacks-or-Better or Double Bonus Poker. It doesn't really matter if they are short-pay machines since all players are competing on the same game.

Two numbers are usually displayed on each screen: playing credits (which start at a large number and are reduced by five for each play) and credits earned (which start at zero and increase as you hit payoffs). A tournament session typically lasts only ten to twenty minutes, so it's very unlikely you will use up all the playing credits. The machines shut off at the end of the allotted time, and the results are recorded by the tournament director. Only the credits earned have any value; remaining playing credits are worthless, so you should play as fast as you can.

The usual mode of play to maximize the EV for each hand is not optimal in this situation. Just getting the "expected" payback is not likely to win a prize, so you have to go for the big payoffs. Further, taking time to think about borderline hands is simply time wasted. Before the tournament starts you must be prepared to go for potential quads, straight flushes and royals. For example:

Hold any pat full house or better.

Hold one pair, trips or quads.

Hold two or more to a straight flush or royal.

Hold a single ten or higher card.

Toss everything else out, including one of two pairs.

Never draw to a straight or flush. One high card, or even a five-card draw has more potential for a big payoff. You might even break a straight or flush to draw to a three-card straight flush. Other tournaments are likely to have different formats, but most of these tips should apply.

One Coin vs. Five Coin Play

Several writers have stated that you should always play the maximum number of coins on any video poker game. Playing fewer coins reduces the payback because you don't qualify for the jackpot payoff on a royal flush. The long-term loss is about 1.5% on Jacks-or-Better, or a bit less on wild card games. It would be heartbreaking to hit a royal and be paid only $62.50 instead of $1,000 (or higher in the case of a progressive jackpot). Many go on to say that it's better to play five coins on a quarter machine than one coin on an otherwise identical dollar machine. Your bet-per-play is roughly the same, but you get the full payoff if you hit a royal.

So far, so good. The problem is that this has been repeated as dogma by gaming columnists who are not very knowledgeable about video poker. The advice is often simplified to the effect that it's always better to play five coins on one machine than one coin on a similar machine of the next higher denomination. The example often given is, in effect, "If you don't want to bet $1.25 per play, then don't play a quarter machine. Instead, find a nickel machine of the same type and always play five coins." This would be good advice if they didn't substitute "same type" for that critical phrase "otherwise identical." To clarify this, consider the following:

Assume for the moment that your game of choice is Jacks-or-Better, but you don't want to wager $1.25 every play. Sure, there are many nickel machines around, but instead of the full-pay 9/6 payoff schedule, most of them have an 8/5 schedule. This is the "same type," but it's not "otherwise identical." True, we would gain 1.5% by playing five coins to qualify for the royal, but that's in the long term. More importantly, the reduced payoff schedule costs us 2.23%, so we not only lose a net .73% but also have larger bankroll fluctuations due to this loss being in the short term!

It's even worse on Deuces Wild. Full-pay Deuces (15/9/5 for five-of-a-kind, straight flush and quads, respectively) will yield about 100.75% payback. Playing fewer than five coins costs about 1.18%, but the 16/10/4 payoff schedule found on many nickel machines costs nearly 6%, so you'd be giving up an additional 4.8% by playing five nickels instead of one quarter!

As you can see, it's not as cut and dried as it's often presented, but to state it as simply as possible: *If you can't find a nickel machine with as good a payoff schedule, you're usually better off playing only one quarter instead of five nickels.*

But that's not to say that I recommend playing only one coin. The purpose of this book is to teach you to be a winner at video poker, and you can't be a long term winner when you play against a house edge. However, you may want to give this advice to a friend who goes with you but isn't a serious player and just wants some low-cost fun. In Las Vegas it's easy to find full-pay quarter machines of almost any kind you like, while there are very few full-pay nickel games.

Please don't get the idea that the above discussion applies only where full-pay games are available. Suppose you are in a casino where the Jacks-or-Better choice is a quarter machine with an 8/5 schedule or a nickel machine with a 6/5 schedule. If we play five nickels instead of one quarter, the reduction by two on the full house costs 2.3% for a net loss of .8%.

However, if the nickel machine has a 7/5 schedule, the loss is only 1.15%, so you gain .35% by playing five nickels instead of one quarter on the 8/5 machine (although you still have slightly larger bankroll fluctuations).

It's rare that a casino has full-pay dollar machines and no full-pay quarter machines; in fact, just the opposite is often the case, so this discussion generally applies only when deciding between nickel and quarter machines.

There is one case where it is actually advantageous to play one quarter rather than five quarters. See the section on the "2nd Chance Progressives" on page 79.

Chapter 9

Probabilities and Random Numbers

How Often a Jackpot?

How often might you expect to hit a royal flush? This depends not only on luck[13] but on how fast you play. An estimate used in one early book is four hands per minute (15 seconds per hand). From my own experience, and from watching others, I felt sure that the typical experienced player is much faster than that. To find out just how fast, I timed myself several times and found that I play anywhere from eight to 15 hands per minute depending on the machine and my mood.

I then watched several other players who seemed to know what they were doing (without letting them know they were being timed). Some were faster (up to 16 hands per minute even while feeding quarters to a noncredit machine), and some were slower, but none played fewer than seven hands per minute. The average was just under nine hands per minute, or about 500 hands per hour after taking a few minutes out for a drink or a pit stop.

One reader claimed the ability to play 400 hands in 15 minutes, but it would require playing two very fast machines to make that possible. It's doubtful that such a rate could be maintained error-free for a significant length of time, but most pros claim playing rates between 600 and 1,000 hands per hour.

---

[13]Oops, I used that word "luck." Yes, luck exists, but it affects your outcome only in the short term. In the long run, it is skill that makes the difference between a winner and a loser. In this author's opinion the word "luck" should be used only in the past tense. It's reasonable to say "I've been lucky" or "I've been unlucky" (either of which is likely in any one session), but this can not be carried into the present. That is, just because I've been lucky doesn't mean that I am lucky or that a particular machine is lucky. And it certainly can't be projected into the future ("I will be lucky" or "I feel lucky today"). A mathematician or statistician will refer to standard deviations rather than luck. Jean Scott, author of *The Frugal Gambler*, has another way to put it: "The more you study, the 'luckier' you will get."

Since the games average one royal in about 37,000 to 48,000 plays, a typical player may expect to average one jackpot for every 50 to 100 hours of play. But note that this is an average, which is meaningful only as a statistical projection. Just because you have played eighty hours doesn't mean you're "due" for a jackpot. Ironically, unskilled players are likely to hit more royals than skilled players because they often try for a royal when there is a better draw available — one with a higher EV.

Regardless of how long you've played or how many jackpots you've hit, you can reasonably expect about four or five royals in your next 400 hours of play. Of course if you play faster or slower than 500 games per hour, your average playing time per jackpot will be shorter or longer, respectively. (See "Probability of a Jackpot (or of No Jackpot)" below for further discussion on this subject.)

How Fast Do You Play?

To measure your own rate of play, first build up some credits on a machine. Then check the starting time on your watch, and drop one quarter into a cup as you make each play. After counting 40 games by dropping a full roll into the cup, check the time, subtract the starting time, and divide 40 by the elapsed time.

For example, if it takes five minutes and 20 seconds (5.33 minutes) to play 40 hands, you are playing at the average rate of 40 ÷ 5.33 = 7.5 games per minute. Multiplying by 60 yields a speed of 450 hands per hour.

Be sure to play at your normal pace when timing yourself; if you try to play fast, you will not only get a false indication of your rate but you also may make costly errors along the way. Better yet, get someone else to time you.

Probability of a Jackpot (or of No Jackpot)

The 19th century French mathematician Siméon Poisson almost certainly never conceived of a game such as video poker, yet he developed a formula to calculate the probability of rare events that is very applicable. His formula, now called the Poisson Distribution, is

$$P = \frac{C^H}{H! \bullet e^C}$$

where P is the probability of H hits (royals) in C cycles, one cycle is the expected average number of plays per hit (about 37,000 to 48,000 plays for various video poker games), and e is the mathematical constant 2.71828, which is used as the base for natural logarithms. No, you don't have dig out your old algebra books; I'll do the math for you.

Suppose you play 40,000 hands (one cycle[14]) with accurate play on a Jacks-or-Better machine. If you played many sessions of 40,000 hands you could expect an average of one royal per session, but what are the probabilities in any one session? Using Poisson's formula, we find:

Royals (Hits) in One Cycle		
H	**P (%)**	**Cumulative %**
0	36.8	36.8
1	36.8	73.6
2	18.4	92.0
3	6.1	98.1
4	1.5	99.6
5	0.3	99.9
6 or more	0.1	100.0

Perhaps you are surprised to learn that the chance of not hitting even one royal in 40,000 plays is equal to chance of hitting exactly one. There is an 18.4% chance of two royals, 6.1% chance of three, and so on. Looking at it another way, there is better than a 63% chance of hitting at least one royal and a 27% chance of two or more royals in 40,000 plays.

---

[14]I should mention that I dislike the use of the word "cycle" with respect to video poker. Some novice players get the idea that since 40,000 hands is said to be one cycle that the machine will yield exactly one royal per 40,000 hands, and once a royal is hit you will have to wait another 40,000 hands for another royal on that particular machine. Nothing could be further from the truth, as we shall see in this section.

Suppose you consider the "long term" to be at least 200,000 plays. That's equivalent to five cycles for this game, so let's see what Poisson tells us about the long term.

Royals (Hits) in Five Cycles		
H	**P (%)**	**Cumulative %**
0	0.7	0.7
1	3.4	4.1
2	8.4	12.5
3	14.0	26.5
4	17.5	44.0
5	17.6	61.6
6	14.6	76.2
7	10.4	86.6
8	8.3	94.9
9 or more	5.1	100.0

Before looking at this it might seem impossible to play 200,000 hands without hitting a royal, yet Poisson tells us that there is a 0.7% probability of this happening (about one chance in 140). And you had better believe it. I once went 160,000 hands without a royal! You "expect" five royals in 200,000 plays, yet the probability of hitting exactly five royals is only 17.6%. However, there's a 23.4% chance of hitting seven or more royals, so it all balances out in the (very) long run.

Another way of looking at it is to ask "What is the probability of *not* hitting a royal in a given amount of play?" With H = 0, Poisson's formula simplifies to $P = \dfrac{1}{e^C}$ so we can quickly generate the following table:

Probability of no Royals in C Cycles	
C	**P (%)**
0	100.0
1	36.8
2	13.5
3	4.98
4	1.83
5	0.67
6	0.25
7	0.09
8	0.03

For example, there is approximately a five percent chance of not getting even one royal in three "cycles" (120,000 hands on Jacks-or-Better).

Money Management — The Mandatory Subject

"Almost every gambling book you read has a big section on this subject. Some of the information can be useful, but much of it is little more than a cruel hoax." —Jean Scott, *The Frugal Gambler*

Most gaming books include a section on money management, and in many cases that's the major thrust of those books, so I would be remiss if I avoided the subject altogether. There is a wide range of opinion about money management. Mathematicians will tell you it's worthless, and every gambler has his own thoughts on the subject.

Many writers claim that money management alone can make you a winner at any game, even when playing against a consistent a house edge. Recommendations typically include dividing your bankroll into daily session "minibankrolls," using progressive betting systems or combination bets, setting stop-loss limits, and so forth. Although some of these tactics may result in making you a small winner more frequently, none of them will improve your chances of getting ahead in the long term. In fact, some even reduce your chances of becoming a long term winner. Instead of traditional "money management" I offer the following recommendations.

Start by selecting a game and denomination appropriate to the size of your current bankroll. I suggest a match that will give you at least a 95% chance at a jackpot, and a 99% chance would be even better. See Table 6 on page 166 for the bankroll necessary for various desired chances of hitting a jackpot.

To accurately determine your risk of ruin requires either calculating the "standard deviation" and applying it properly to the game in question or doing a Monte Carlo simulation appropriate to the game. See "Determining Bankroll Requirements" on page 125 and "Probability of Ruin" on page 127 for more information. Even better might be the actual experience of professional players.

How Big a Bankroll Do You Need?

In the "Money Management" section I said that it's important to not overplay your bankroll. So just how big a bankroll is necessary to have a reasonable chance of surviving for the long term? And just what is meant by a "reasonable" chance?

Let's take a close look at the long term and try to determine the bankroll necessary to hit a royal flush. It will now be necessary to include all payoffs except the royal because we must start with enough money to give us a reasonable chance at that jackpot.

Excluding only the royal flush, the payback with accurate play on a full-pay Jacks-or-Better machine is about 97.5%. Thus, a $1,000 bankroll on a 25¢ Jacks-or-Better should provide about 32,000 plays.

$$\frac{\$1000}{\$1.25} = 800 \text{ bets} \quad \text{and} \quad \frac{800}{1 - .975} = 32,000$$

We must resist the temptation to simply divide 32,000 by 40,000 and say that we have an 80% chance of a jackpot. We did this with a small bankroll and got a reasonable approximation because the probabilities are nearly linear at low levels, but the error becomes too great at higher levels for such simplification.

To put this in perspective, a bankroll of $3,000 should provide nearly 100,000 plays, but although we can reasonably *expect* two or three royals in that many plays, there still is no certainty of hitting even one (see "Probability of a Jackpot (or of No Jackpot)" on page 119). Actually, the $1,000 bankroll gives us roughly a 60% chance of hitting at least one jackpot (see Table 6 on page 166 or use the Poisson formula). If you want to know how Table 6 was generated, see the section "Determining Bankroll Requirements" on page 125 You should also read the Risk of Ruin, Volatility Index and Attractiveness Quotient sections in this book.

Excluding the natural royal flush, the payback with Precision Play on a full-pay Deuces Wild is just under 99%, so a starting bankroll of $1,000 should provide more than 75,000 plays, giving you about an 80% chance of a jackpot. The same $1,000 bankroll on a Joker Wild would yield only about 47,000 plays and a 65% chance of a jackpot. This pretty much spans the range, so we can see that a starting bankroll equal to the basic royal flush jackpot will give us about a 60 to 80% chance of hitting at least one royal on most of the recommended games.

Does this mean that, of the "flat top" games (that is, games with a nonprogressive jackpot), we should play only the Deuces Wild? The answer is a qualified "yes," since a large bankroll gives a better chance of a jackpot on Deuces Wild than on any of the other games, except for full pay Jacks-or-Better with a bonus on quads or lower hands or a full pay Double Double Jackpot machine (see Appendix E on page 180). Remember, however, that the greater volatility of the Deuces Wild (due to the relatively infrequent occurrence of the four deuces "minijackpot") causes larger fluctuations in your bankroll.

Table 6 lists the starting bankroll necessary for any reasonable desired chance of hitting a royal flush on some of the most common games. As pointed out earlier, the necessary bankroll goes up *faster* than your desired probability of hitting a royal. No amount of money or playing time can guarantee a jackpot, just as no system (other than owning the several house advantages) can guarantee a win in any gambling situation.

Of course you can increase your chances of a royal flush by drawing to it in more cases than recommended by Precision Play, but the frequency of small wins will decrease, costing you money in the long run. If you intend to visit the casino only once or twice in your lifetime, or if you prefer gambling over playing the best odds and being a long term winner, then throw this book away, and draw to the royal at every opportunity.

Determining Bankroll Requirements

Skip this section if you don't like mathematics. You'll be able to determine your bankroll needs just by referring to Table 6 in most cases. The purpose of this section is to show how the table for bankroll requirements was developed.

To understand the calculations, let's start out by looking at a simple situation, one that everyone is familiar with — dice. What are the chances of throwing a four on a single die? (We are assuming here that the dice are honest.) Since the die has six sides, each with equal probability of coming up, the chance of getting a four in a single throw with a die is 1-in-6, or $\frac{1}{6}$.

But what are the chances of getting a four at least once in two throws? Many people would simply add $\frac{1}{6}$ plus $\frac{1}{6}$ and say the probability is $\frac{1}{3}$, and this is a reasonable approximation in this case. This reasoning, however, would suggest that we are certain to roll exactly one four in six throws, and you would only have to try it a couple times yourself to see that this is simply not true. To correctly determine the probability of at least one four, we must calculate the probability of its not occurring, and subtract that from certainty, or one.

The chance of a four not occurring in one throw is $\frac{5}{6}$, so the chance of not occurring in either of two throws is $(\frac{5}{6}) \times (\frac{5}{6})$. Subtracting from one (certainty), the chance of a four occurring at least once in two throws is $1-[(\frac{5}{6}) \times (\frac{5}{6})] = \frac{11}{36}$. Note that this is a little less than the $\frac{1}{3}$ approximation above.

In three throws, the probability of at least one four is $1-(\frac{5}{6})^3$, and in n throws, the probability is $1-(\frac{5}{6})^n$.

In general, then, the probability, P, of a given event occurring *at least once* in n tries is

$$P = 1 - (1 - p)^n$$

where p is the probability of it occurring on each try.

Now back to video poker jackpots. Let's start with some definitions:

PR	The probability of hitting a royal flush in one play
DP	The desired probability of hitting a royal flush
n	The number of plays
BR	Our bankroll (expressed as a number of plays)
PB	The long-term payback of the machine, *excluding the royal*
LNP	The likely number of plays with a given bankroll
ln	Natural logarithm

Our goal is to determine the bankroll necessary to have a desired probability, DP, of hitting a jackpot. From the preceding discussion we see that

$$DP = 1 - (1 - PR)^n$$

However, DP is given, and we need to determine n, so we'll rearrange this equation to

$$(1 - PR)^n = 1 - DP$$

and then take the natural logarithm of both sides, resulting in

$$n \cdot \ln(1 - PR) = \ln(1 - DP)$$

which, when solved for n, results in the formula

$$n = \frac{\ln(1 - DP)}{\ln(1 - PR)}$$

As we saw in the chapters on the "Short Run," the likely number of plays with a given bankroll is

$$LNP = \frac{BR}{1 - PB}$$

which we will rearrange to express the bankroll required to last for a desired number of plays as

$$BR = (1 - PB) \cdot LPN$$

Substituting n above for LNP, we get the formula we're looking for:

$$BR = \frac{(1 - PB) \cdot \ln(1 - DP)}{\ln(1 - PR)}$$

Let's take an example. Suppose we have determined that a particular game's payback (excluding the royal flush) is 97.5% (.975), that the probability of a royal each play is one in 40,000 (.000025), and that we want a 60% chance of hitting that jackpot. How big a bankroll do we need? Substituting these figures into the above formula, we get

$$BR = \frac{(1-0.975) \bullet \ln(1-0.60)}{\ln(1-0.000025)} = \frac{0.025 \bullet \ln(0.40)}{\ln(0.999975)} = \frac{-0.0229}{-0.000025} = 916$$

Remember, however, that BR is a number of plays, so it must be multiplied by the size of the wager to get a dollar amount. Thus, on a five-coin quarter machine, we would need a bankroll of 916 x $1.25 = $1,145.

It's interesting to note that on this hypothetical machine, as on many real games, a starting bankroll equal to the size of the jackpot will yield only about a 60% chance of hitting that jackpot at least once.

The above analysis applies only to relatively large bankrolls, due to the concentration of large payoffs on infrequent hands. For other ways to look at the chance of ruin, continue reading through the following sections.

Probability of Ruin

Table 6 on page 166 tells us the bankroll needed for a given desired chance of hitting a jackpot (royal flush). This table also can be used backwards to find the approximate chance of hitting a jackpot with a given bankroll. For example, suppose we have a $2,000 bankroll with which we intend to play standard full-pay quarter Jacks-or-Better.

Going across the 25¢ J-or-B (9/6) line, we see that $2,000 falls somewhere between the amounts in the columns for 75% and 90% chance of a jackpot, so we could estimate roughly an 80% chance of hitting a jackpot before we are beset by gambler's ruin. Don't be disturbed by that term. "Ruin" simply means losing our predetermined starting bankroll. (But if you don't quit playing at that point then you are a candidate for Gamblers Anonymous.)

Looked at another way, we can subtract the 80% chance of success from one and find that we have a 20% chance of ruin. This is a close enough approximation if our desire is to play until we either hit a royal or go broke. But what if we want to know our chance of ruin more accurately?

The probability of ruin in a game with even money payoffs is given by the formula:

$$P = \frac{\left(\dfrac{1+A}{1-A}\right)^{W} - 1}{\left(\dfrac{1+A}{1-A}\right)^{W+C} - 1}$$

Where: P = Probability of Ruin

             A = Player's Advantage

            W = Amount desired to win

            C = Starting Capital

As in all our formulae, W and C are in betting units (e.g., multiple of $1.25 for a 25¢ machine). This can best be explained with an example.

Suppose we have a $200 bankroll and decide to play until we either lose it or win $100. Thus, our starting capital is C = $200 ÷ $1.25 = 160 betting units, and the desired win amount is W = $100 ÷ $1.25 = 80 betting units.

If we play the 25¢ super-full-pay 10/6 Jacks-or-Better, our advantage is .65% or .0065. Plugging all these numbers into the formula, we find the probability of ruin is about .0845 or 8.45%, so we have a 91.55% chance of winning $100 before we lose $200.

If we decide that we'll never quit unless we go broke, then W is in effect infinite, and the formula simplifies to:

$$P = \left(\frac{1-A}{1+A}\right)^{C}$$

Suppose in the above example we decided not to stop, but rather to keep playing until we either lose the $200 (plus any winnings along the way) or amass a vast fortune. We would then use this latter formula and find that the chance of ruin is about 12.5%, or roughly 50% greater than it was with a win limit of half our bankroll.

What if we have a much larger bankroll? Obviously, the bigger the starting bankroll in relation to the bet size, the less our chance of ruin. For example, starting with a $5,000 bankroll on $1 Deuces Wild, this formula indicates that the chance of ruin would be only .005%.

We must use caution, however, in applying these formulae. If we were tossing a perfectly balanced coin and betting even money on tails every throw, our advantage would be zero. Suppose instead that we were tossing a coin that is slightly heavier on the heads side (as many coins are), making tails a little more likely to come up. Further, let's suppose that the imbalance is such that the probability of tails is 0.50325, thus giving us the same 0.65% advantage as on a 10/6 Jacks-or-Better video poker. In this case, the above calculations would apply accurately since the payoff is always even money. In video poker, however, the wide range of payoffs and their probabilities make such formulae useful only for the very long term.

More recently, a new formula that accurately takes into account the wide range of probabilities and paybacks of some games was developed by Russian mathematician Evgeny Sorokin and published on the website jbmath.com. Game analyst Jazbo Burns adapted it to video poker, and it was published in the March/April, 1999 issue of *Video Poker Times*, but the math was considered too complex for this book. In the September/October issue of *VPT* TomSki used the formula to create a table giving the risk of ruin for a variety of attractive games with various starting bankrolls. For details on the formula's development and application, refer to the Fall, 1999 *Blackjack Forum*.

So far we have discussed the risk in playing video poker mostly from a theoretical point of view based on various calculations. Besides the formulae in these sections, the Volatility Index (VI), a standard deviation calculation that takes the variations of the payoff schedule into account, has been discussed in detail elsewhere in this book. Some readers of earlier works complained that the math went over their heads, and others felt that the risk was actually much greater or much less than implied by the formulae and charts. What seemed to be needed was a table where a player could, with confidence, just look up the risk of ruin.

To get a clear picture from a very practical point of view, a Monte Carlo simulation was done to determine the real risk of ruin. (For those who aren't familiar with the Monte Carlo analysis method, it's simply the use of random numbers to "play" millions of hands and tabulate the results.) This has been done for several of the most popular games, and Table 7 on page 167 gives the results such a simulation for standard full-pay Deuces Wild. Similar tables for other games have been published in *Video Poker Times*.

Let's take an example to see how to use this table. Suppose you decide to play a five-coin 25¢ Deuces Wild for four hours or until you lose a $125 starting bankroll. You play 500 hands per hour. The intersection of 100 bets ($125 at $1.25 per bet) and 2,000 plays (four hours at 500 hands per hour) in Table 7 indicates a 53% chance of losing the entire $125. If this were repeated many times, you would make an average of 1,490 plays and end up with an average gain of 11 bets per session. (The game's 100.75% expected return figures out to a gain of 11.2 bets after 1,490 plays, so this is right on target.)

It's interesting to scan across one line of the table. Starting with 200 bets, for example, there is almost no risk of ruin in up to 1,000 plays. In 2,000 plays, the risk climbs to 13%, and at 4,000 plays, it's up to 37%. Even with unlimited play, however, the risk of ruin levels out and never climbs above about 75%. Remember, however, that "ruin" means the loss of your *entire* starting bankroll, so just because you avoid ruin, it doesn't mean that you did not lose some or most of that bankroll.

Similarly, let's scan down one column. If you have time to play 4,000 hands, then you have a 93% risk of losing a 25-bet starting bankroll. Starting with 50 bets reduces the risk to 85%, and starting with 100 bets cuts it to 70%. There is only a 37% chance of losing 200 bets, and starting with about 500 bets cuts the risk of ruin almost to zero — assuming we quit after 4,000 plays as we had planned, regardless of whether we are ahead or behind.

Now let's look at a practical application. Suppose you are going to Las Vegas for a weekend with a $500 gambling bankroll. Your game is standard 25¢ Deuces Wild which you play very accurately. You plan to play for a total of about 16 hours in sessions of about two hours each. You estimate your playing speed at 500 hands per hour.

Conventional money management advice would be to divide the $500 by the anticipated eight sessions, and put only $62.50 (50 bets at $1.25 each) in your pocket for each session. You have already decided to limit each session to two hours (1,000 plays) so the chart shows a 64% risk of ruin (probability of losing the entire $62.50) in each session. The probability of ruin on every one of eight consecutive such sessions is $(.64)^8$ or about 2.8%, so you have better than a 97% probability of leaving with at least part of your bankroll intact (and hopefully more than you started with). Note that the mean ending bankroll is 55 bets for an average gain of five bets per session. Thus your total expected win is 8 x 5 x $1.25 = $50.00. Perhaps more important to you, since you're only here for a weekend, is that you get to make an average of only 640 plays per session, so each session is likely to end after about one and a quarter hours instead of the anticipated two hours.

Now let's set that conventional "wisdom" aside and take the entire $500 (or whatever we have at the time) along on each session. That is, let's consider the entire trip to be a single playing session. The intersection of 400 bets and 8,000 plays shows a 21% risk of ruin, so you would have only a 79% probability of leaving with at least part of your bankroll. The mean ending bankroll, however, is 458 bets so you have an expected gain of 58 x $1.25 = $72.50. The mean expected playing time is about 7490 ÷ 500 = 15 hours, so you may still lose your $500 and be forced to quit playing sooner than you would like, but your playing time is not cut nearly as short as it would be if you divided your bankroll into eight parts.

So did the money management system help? Well, it reduced your risk of ruin, but it did so simply by reducing your playing time. Instead of playing for 16 hours as you had planned, your expected total playing time is only about ten hours. You have only a 2.8% risk of total ruin, but your expected win is only $50.00. On the other hand, if you played with your entire bankroll at stake at all times you would have a 21% risk of ruin — but your expected win would be $72.50. The net effect of the "money management" scheme was to give up nearly a third of your expected winnings and several hours of fun. That doesn't sound like a good trade-off to me. You're better off just taking your predetermined bankroll along and playing your best at all times *provided you don't overplay your bankroll*. That is, you should not be playing $1 machines with only a $500 bankroll.

Of course you might feel that the reduction in risk of ruin makes the "minibankroll" system worthwhile. After all, there's a big difference between 21% and 2.8% risk. However, this doesn't tell the whole story. First of all, remember that your playing time was cut to only ten hours (5,000 hands). If we interpolate between the risk at 4,000 hands (eight hours) and 8,000 hands (16 hours), we could estimate a risk of about 6.5% to 7% for 5,000 hands. And second, none of these risk figures say how much money you're likely to have left if you don't lose it all. In summary, the "minibankroll" scheme only makes a trade-off between expected gain and risk of ruin.

This has been one player's situation. Yours is probably different, and you should work through the numbers for your own case.

How the Games Were Analyzed

This discussion is for the reader who is curious about how the playing strategies were developed. Again, if you're not mathematically inclined, just skip this chapter. Ignoring the derivation will not affect the accuracy of your play or reduce your expectation in any way.

Okay, you want the details, so we'll start with the basics. With a standard 52-card deck, as in Jacks-or-Better and Deuces Wild, any book on draw poker will tell you that there are exactly 2,598,960 possible five-card hands before the draw. (For the mathematically inclined, that's the combinations of 52 items taken five at a time.) For each of these starting hands, you can discard and draw up to five new cards.

If you draw one card, there are five possible discards, and the card you don't hold will be replaced with one of the 47 cards remaining in the deck, so there are 5 x 47 = 235 possible new results after a one-card draw.

If you draw two cards, there are ten possible combinations of discards, each with 1,081 possible draws (47 items taken two at a time). A three-card draw again has ten discard combinations, but each has 16,215 possible outcomes. There are only five possible four-card draws, but each has 178,365 possible results.

Finally, there are 1,533,939 possible results from a five-card re-draw. Thus, although there are still only 2,598,960 possible final hands, there are nearly *seven trillion* possible ways of getting there.

Adding the joker to the deck increases the number of possible hands to 2,869,685 for Joker Wild, with a similar increase in the number of possible paths to a final hand.

How can such complex games possibly be analyzed? The first step is predraw hand analysis; that is, given a starting hand, examine *every possible* draw to determine the best way to play the hand and the EV for that play.

In my original program, written in 1991, analyzing one predraw hand took the computer anywhere from a fraction of a second for a one-card draw to about an hour for a zilch hand requiring a five-card draw. My latest program will analyze all 32 possible ways to play any hand in a few milliseconds. There are at least two commercially available programs that will do the same thing in less than one second.

Hands that cannot be improved (such as a low straight flush or four-of-a-kind) obviously do not need a computer run, but most predraw hands require several runs to average out the effects of various discards. In such cases an analysis must be run on anywhere from two to dozens of similar hands for each entry in Tables 2 – 5.

Even some hands that most people would simply take for granted must be tested; for example, the full house must be analyzed to see if it's more profitable to discard the pair and draw for four-of-a-kind. (On Jacks-or-Better it is if there is a quads jackpot of at least 136-for-1, or $170 on a five-coin 25¢ machine).

Suppose you are drawing to a suited king and queen when none of the discards is of the same suit but one of the discards is a high card. We would not need the computer to observe that only one royal flush, one straight flush, and two possible four-of-a-kind hands can result. You might even have arrived at the numbers of other final hands with a few minutes work on a pocket calculator. But this is only one of several hundred predraw hands that were examined in order to create Table 2, and one of the simpler cases at that.

To get an accurate evaluation, you must consider the case where one of the discards was a nine, ten or ace, or where one of them was of the same suit as the king-queen. Such discards would reduce the EV slightly by eliminating some possible straights or flushes (see "What Is A Penalty Card?" on page 28).

Many other types of hands, such as an inside straight with two or fewer high cards, were tested but omitted from the table because their EV is less than the .359 EV of a five-card redraw.

Without the computer, generating Table 2 would have been a formidable task, and extending the calculations to accurately build the table in "The Payoff Schedule — Jacks-or-Better" might have been a lifetime project.

Once Table 2 had been generated we had a working strategy that would allow extracting very nearly the maximum possible wins from the machine. The final step was to reduce the hand rank table to the Precision Play rules so that anyone would be able to play accurately in an actual casino situation.

Some authors promise 99.6% payback for this game, but several independent analyses have shown that *the absolute maximum payback with computer-perfect play* is 99.544% (apparently rounded up from 99.5439%). My 99.53% figure is a realistic and achievable payback with the easy-to-use Precision Play rules, but 99.6% is impossible unless there is something wrong with the machine.

Random Numbers and Gaming Regulations

As often stated, the calculations in this book are based upon the premise that the cards are dealt completely at random, with each card having an equal probability of occurring, just as if a standard deck of playing cards had been thoroughly shuffled. It's likely that you already know that all video gaming machines (and nearly all reel slots) are actually digital computers with fancy displays. Since a computer can be made to control its output any way the programmer desires, it could easily be set up to restrict the frequency of certain hands and thus set the payback to any level desired.

This is not just theory. An article in the December, 1992 issue of *Blackjack Forum* reported that certain 21 machines that were produced outside of this country had great rules and bonus payouts and thus appeared to be very favorable to the player, yet they could be set to pay back anywhere from 84 to 99% by internal switches. A video poker machine could just as easily be programmed to reduce the payback, for example by reducing the probability of some cards. But relax — I have never received a report of any such machines in any major U.S. gambling jurisdiction.

Such a deceptive reduction in the payback is highly unlikely in Nevada where regulations (see Appendix D on page 176) require that all gaming machines determine the outcome in a strictly random manner. We are told that the program chips are thoroughly tested by Nevada Gaming Control, and that they do spot checks to look for any machine that has an illegal chip. The casino could be subject to a large fine or potentially even loss of its gaming license if a machine was found to be intentionally biased.

The blackjack machines mentioned above are currently in use in other countries, however, so it's reasonable to assume that similarly dishonest video poker is also offered in such areas.

At least one nonrandom video poker game has shown up in an Indian casino in an Eastern seaboard state that apparently doesn't require and test for randomness. There may be no such requirement in any Indian casino, although I have been told that the only Indian casino in Nevada at this time (the Avi Casino south of Laughlin) has voluntarily agreed to be bound by Nevada regulations.

All I can say is that you must use extreme caution when playing where regulations are lax, especially if the payoff schedule seems too good to be true.

Even in well regulated jurisdictions you will often notice a machine running in apparent cycles, making many payoffs then going "cold" for quite awhile. Is this due to intentional biases? Probably not. It's impossible for a digital computer to generate truly random numbers. Instead, they utilize a pseudo-random number generator. Such a program generates a very long sequence of numbers that, while not perfectly random from a statistician's point of view, meet the criteria of randomness as well or better than a deck of cards being shuffled by hand. The sequence typically runs for many trillions of numbers before it repeats.

One of the best types of algorithmic pseudo-random number generators is called "multiplicative-congruential." In this method, a seed number is multiplied by a constant, and the result is divided by another very large constant (usually a prime number, and certainly prime with respect to the multiplier). The remainder of this division becomes the new "random" number, and it's also used as the seed for the next iteration.

Whether this or some other type of generator is used, it is almost certainly random enough so that the long-term payback of the machine is within a tiny fraction of one percent of our predictions. According to *American Casino Guide* (see Appendix F on page 186) the IGT machines use a random number generator with about 16,000,000,000,000,000,000 possible outcomes (apparently a 64-bit algorithm). Although it does not say how these are mapped into the 52 (or 53) possible cards, this should generate a random sequence of cards that could be predicted only with the use of a computer running the same algorithm, and even then it would be necessary to somehow know what point the RNG was currently in its cycle.

However, even truly random numbers would not preclude the possibility of short-term clumping of numbers that can result in apparent hot and cold cycles. There is some discussion of the possible effects of this clumping in "Questions and Answers" on page 142. The key word here, though, is "apparent" since there is no way to know when such a clump would begin or end.

In Nevada and Louisiana, and probably in New Jersey, you can play in confidence that the machines are not intentionally biased. Let's hope that similar regulations are soon adopted for other states and Indian gaming.

Our best protection is probably the fact that Nevada regulations also require any company selling machines in Nevada to certify that all machines they sell *anywhere* meet Nevada regulations but that would not preclude unscrupulous management in an unregulated casino from replacing the program chip with a biased program after the machine was delivered. You should avoid any game whose rules or payoff schedule appear to be too good to be true (they almost certainly are). Personally, I would not play anything in a casino where any game appeared to be too good to be true.

Chapter 10

Cheating

Cheating is possible in any type of game. Some people on both sides of all types of competition have worked hard to devise ways to cheat their opponents. In most cases these people could have gained more by expending the same effort honestly. The question here, however, is whether cheating occurs on either side of video poker play.

Obviously, since any video machine is basically a special purpose digital computer, it could be made to do whatever the programmer wanted. Most computers that we work with at home or in business are programmed by software. That is, the program is in read/write memory and is loaded from disk each time it is run. This makes it easy to change the program. The program in a video machine, on the other hand, is stored in a PROM chip (Programmable Read Only Memory), so changing the program requires physically replacing a chip on the circuit board. This makes it nearly impossible to reprogram a video machine without leaving hard evidence. Since Nevada Gaming Control does random checks, pulling the program chip and comparing it with the approved program, such a change would be very risky for a casino.

I have heard of only one case of such cheating, and this was a slot route company that, in 1989, had modified the program chip in machines they installed in bars to never hit a royal flush. That company was soon out of business and its principals facing criminal charges. I have also heard of one five-joker machine that appeared to be nonrandom, but this was in an Indian casino in an Eastern state where it was probably not illegal due to the lack of regulation.

For more information, you should read *American Casino Guide* by Steve Bourie, especially the chapter "Are Slot machines Honest?" (see Appendix F on page 186). My opinion is that video poker may currently be the most honest gambling game available in this country.

And is there cheating on the player's side? I have never heard of anyone successfully cheating at video poker other than by taking advantage of a malfunctioning machine (see the next section), feeding counterfeit bills into the bill acceptor, or using home-made "slugs" that resemble tokens.

There are several ways, however, that players may attempt to cheat during a promotion. For example, if there is a hand-paid bonus on quads, an unethical player might play a multi-game machine and fake playing off the bonus hand by switching to another game. He then switches back when a different floorperson is nearby to claim a second payoff for the same bonus hand. This could be dangerous, as the player could be 86'd or perhaps even prosecuted for felony fraud if the deception were detected. Remember, the floor personnel are not stupid, and there are security cameras everywhere in a casino.

Machine Malfunctions

I am frequently asked if a video poker machine is ever "broken" in such a way that it reduces the payback. I am happy to report that I have never heard of such a case other than bad buttons that make it difficult to maintain both speed and accuracy. It is extremely unlikely that the electronics would malfunction and yet leave the game playable. The electronic components are much more reliable than the mechanical parts, and most machines do a self test each time they restart after the door has been opened.

However, I have personally experienced two cases where a machine malfunction favored the player. Both of these were due to mechanical failure of an internal switch. One of the machines was a "coin dropper" (no credit play), so it was necessary to feed five coins for each play. Sometimes when I thought I had dropped in five coins, the machine would drop one back into the coin return and go ahead and start the hand showing a five-coin bet on the screen. After a while I realized that the switch in the coin comparator mechanism was bouncing and sometimes counting up two credits for one coin. I estimated that this was happening about once per 15 coins inserted, giving me an extra six or seven percent edge.

The other case involved the switch that tells the machine when a coin has been fed out of the hopper. When a machine is paying out, the hopper does not pick up a coin on every cycle, so the coins are counted just as they drop out into the tray. In this particular machine, that switch was obviously not making good contact, and an average of about one coin in five was not being counted as it dropped. This gave the player a fantastic 25% edge!

As it happened, both of these machines were in a casino where I was on very good terms with a slot shift manager, so I reported them directly to him. What I didn't know at the time is that in Nevada it is a crime to knowingly take advantage of a malfunctioning machine. I'm glad now that this didn't happen in another casino; I might have continued playing and subjected myself to possible prosecution if my activity had been detected.

If you encounter such a machine it will be up to your own personal morals and/or concern of detection as to what you do about it. My recommendation is to report it immediately to a slot attendant.

Another situation that I witnessed occurred when a local casino opened a new wing. I initially passed by a bank of Deuces Wild five-way progressives because of a short pay schedule, but then I noticed several pros playing furiously. A closer look revealed that the progressive counters were not resetting when hit, so they just kept growing. The result was that the payback was over 105% at the time and climbing. This lasted all night until the slot engineers came in and shut down the bank so the problem could be corrected. I never got a chance to play. I don't know if this would be considered taking advantage of a machine malfunction since the problem was in the linking computer rather than in the machines themselves. The machines were functioning correctly according to the payoffs shown on the screen.

I have heard of similar situations when new casinos opened. Such errors may be the origin of rumors about new machines being "looser" when a casino opens. In any case, you might want to be near the front of the line when a new casino opens its doors. Or you might prefer to steer clear of any possible brush with the law and avoid playing under such circumstances.

Tipping

Large jackpots are paid by hand. Often the money is counted out to you by the same friendly change person who sold you the roll of coins or gave you five twenties for your $100 bill, with a slot attendant and possibly a security guard standing by. After hitting a jackpot that must be hand paid, most players tip the change person and the slot attendant, especially if they hit a larger than usual jackpot.

This is not a requirement, of course, but keep in mind that these people are generally paid only slightly above minimum wage. Like food servers, valet attendants and other service people, they depend on tokes (tips) for a significant part of their income. If these people have been pleasant and helpful, you may want to show your appreciation.

I once observed a player hit a progressive jackpot for $1,935.00 on a 25¢ Jacks-or-Better machine. When it was paid off, he tipped the change person and the floor person a total of $40. His friend, who had been playing beside him, remarked "You just gave away over two percent of your jackpot. That completely wiped out your advantage in the game." The generous player replied "I'm happy; they're happy. Why worry?"

Did the player actually give up his entire advantage, which had resulted from the large progressive jackpot? The way his friend figured, it would seem so; but let's look closer. The actual net result of the toke was to reduce the $1,935 jackpot to $1,895, thus reducing the total long-term payback from 101.84% to 101.74%. True, a tip cuts into your winnings, but in this case it cut the payback not by two percent but by about one-tenth of one percent.

Security

When you hit a jackpot, it's usually paid in cash and in public view. Although problems are rare, that's an open invitation to muggers and pickpockets. Unfortunately, there is an element of society that wants what you have but doesn't want to put the time and effort into working for it. The casinos are aware of this, and they are always willing to assist you to avoid such a disaster.

One possibility is to take the cash immediately to the casino cage. Some casinos have safe deposit boxes; with others you can just deposit it as in a bank and get a receipt to draw on it later. A security guard will escort you if you ask. If you're staying in the hotel, you can also take your cash to the registration desk and ask them to put it in the safe. In this case, put the money in an envelope, seal the envelope, and sign your name on it. That way, anyone watching when you pick it up just sees an envelope instead of a stack of cash.

If you don't want to leave the money in the casino, ask a security guard to escort you to your car or to a taxi. Some security guards may not be allowed to accept tips, but it wouldn't hurt to offer if you're so inclined.

As it should be anytime you're in or near a crowd of people, never carry a large amount of cash in your wallet in a back trouser pocket, a jacket pocket (even an inside jacket pocket), or a purse. Those are the easiest targets for pickpockets. Most high-stakes players carry their bankroll in a front trouser pocket, rolled up with a rubber band. It's also a good idea to keep your wallet in a front trouser pocket. Ladies should not carry a handbag without a shoulder strap. Even if your wallet or purse holds little cash, you don't want the inconvenience of losing your identification and credit cards. And never, never put your purse down between machines. Not only is there a chance you might forget it, but also, you're giving someone on the other side of the machine a golden opportunity to reach across and snatch it away.

This is not to imply that there are more pickpockets and thieves in Las Vegas or Atlantic City than in other cities. However, there are more people carrying around large amounts of cash, and more crowds with people bumping into one another, making any gambling center a good shopping ground for such people. Why take unnecessary chances?

IRS Reports and Tax Records

The casino is required by IRS regulations to file a form W-2G report whenever they pay a slot jackpot of $1,200 or more. This, of course, requires identification, your social security number and your signature in order to collect the payoff. This obviously is the reason for the jackpots on nonprogressives being increased to 4,700 coins ($1,175 on a 25¢ machine). There are even some machines with jackpots up to 4,796 coins ($1,199), coming even closer to the $1,200 threshold.

On very large jackpots, or if you are not a U.S. citizen, the casino may be required to withhold part of the money for income tax. Of course you are required by law to report all gambling wins on your tax return. However, as of this writing, if you itemize you can deduct documented gambling losses (up to the amount of gambling wins), so you should keep an accurate log of all gains and losses.

With such a log, you may be able to document losses equal to the gains.

We have been told that the log should document each playing session with the following information:

Date and time,

Casino name and location,

The name(s) of anyone with you,

The game type, machine number and denomination,

The amount of win or loss.

Supporting documentation, such as appropriately dated airline tickets, hotel bills, cancelled checks, ATM receipts, restaurant receipts and casino records can also be helpful in case of an audit. (See Appendix F on page 186 for reference material.)

This should not be construed as tax advice. We are not in the business of giving legal advice, nor are we licensed to do so. Besides, tax laws and/or IRS regulations may change between the time this is published and the time you read it. The best policy is to consult an accountant or tax attorney for information on your tax liability and how best to keep records to document your wins and losses.

Questions and Answers

Here I will attempt to tie up any loose strings. Many of these questions have been answered in the text, but they are brought up again here because they are frequently asked. (I would appreciate feedback regarding your own experiences, observations and ideas on these or any similar subjects, or any supporting or conflicting evidence regarding anything in this book. Such input will be useful in updates of this book.)

Q. Is it really possible to be a winner in the long run at video poker?

A. Yes. By selecting a game that offers a potential return exceeding 100% and by always making the play recommended in the strategy, you can come within a few hundredths of one percent of the maximum payback of any video poker game. This will give you a real edge over the house.

Q. You say I can come within a few hundredths of one percent on the game's maximum payback. Can't I get the game's entire rated payback?

A. As explained in "What Does 'Optimum Play' Really Mean?" it is not possible to achieve absolutely perfect play for most games. If you follow the Precision Play rules you will achieve very nearly the highest practical payback for the game.

Q. Precision Play? That still sounds like work, and I just want to have some fun. Can I have fun and win, too?

A. Actually it isn't hard at all. The Precision Play rules make it very easy for several of the most common games. And isn't it more fun when you have a better chance of winning?

Q. Do I have to learn to count cards?

A. No. Each hand is dealt independently from a freshly "shuffled" (randomized) deck, so you only have to select the best cards to hold for each play. In that way, it's similar to playing blackjack with basic strategy. The difference is that you are doing as good as the best blackjack card counter because no card-counting strategy can yield a higher payback for video poker.

Q. You say I must select a good game. How will I know a good game when I see it?

A. Nevada gaming regulations require that each unseen card have the same probability of appearing. Since each machine must display its complete characteristics in the form of a payoff table, either on the glass front or on the screen, all you have to do is look for a payoff schedule that matches the one in the book or cue card.

Q. Where can I find these games?

A. Appendix C on page 172 lists several casinos in southern Nevada. Also, *Video Poker Times* will keep you up to date with reports from all over the country, and you will sometimes find some current good opportunities mentioned on the "Tips" page of my web site and in other web sites.

Q. What if there are none of the recommended games in my area. Can I still be a winner?

A. Unfortunately no system can make it possible to beat any game in the long run when the odds are against you. However, if you are going to play anyway, you can cut your losses to the minimum possible for the available game and get the best chance to be a winner in any particular playing session.

Q. Do you expect more good games to become available outside southern Nevada?

A. Yes. As legal gambling grows and competition continues to build, casinos in many areas are being forced to improve their offerings. I am already getting reports of such occurrences in unexpected places such as in Illinois, Missouri and Iowa. Even some Indian casinos have full pay Jacks-or-Better, and although this game offers "only" 99.54% payback it's much better than anything else around.

Q. How is it possible for the casinos to offer games with over 100% payback? If they can be beaten so easily, why doesn't the casino lose money on them and take them out?

A. Video poker is a very popular game, and only a very small percentage of players expend the small price and effort to learn an accurate strategy. With my publications you can be one of that exclusive few. The vast majority of players make many errors using "intuitive" play or hunches, thus reducing their achieved payback by about two to four percent on the average, so the casino makes a profit in spite of the few good players.

Q. But haven't some casinos taken out or changed certain games because they were losing money on them?

A. Yes, this has happened several times. Examples include the 17/10 Loose Deuces at Lady Luck Casino and the Joker Wild (Two Pair) at Palace Station and the Fiesta, all in Las Vegas. Sometimes a machine manufacturer makes a mistake in calculating a game's payback. The professionals soon analyze it and find it offers over 1.5% positive expectation, so they hit it hard while it lasts. Since the recreational players don't get a chance to play that particular game, the casino loses money on it and soon either replaces the machines or cuts the payoff schedule. Often the casino overreacts, cutting it too much, and nobody plays it any more. Because of this effect, most of the games I recommend offer paybacks in the range of 100.1% to 101.3%. They have found a place in the casino because so few people actually know how to play them correctly. The bottom line in the casino's books gets printed in black and they're satisfied that they have a winner.

Q. Will I win every time I play video poker?

A. Of course not. No one, not even the casino, wins on every playing session. Most people win occasionally at any game they play. If they didn't, they would quit playing; the casinos know this and structure the games to allow occasional big winners. With our methods, you will be able to gain an edge that will make you a favorite to win in the long run.

Q. How big a bankroll do I need?

A. That depends on the game and the denomination, but it has been covered quite extensively in this book. Go back and read the bankroll and risk sections.

Q. What if I'm really serious about winning at video poker?

A. Then you should subscribe to *Video Poker Times*, and you should use cue cards when you are playing any game if you haven't memorized the strategy.

Q. It says that your cue cards give the strategy as a hand rank table. What is that?

A. Many card combinations that are dealt as your first five cards can be played several ways. For example, Q♣ J♣ 10♥ 9♣ 4♣ (in any order) can be played as a four-card straight (holding Q♣ J♣ 10♥ 9♣), a four-card flush (Q♣ J♣ 9♣ 4♣), a three-card inside straight flush (Q♣ J♣ 9♣) or a two-card royal flush (Q♣ J♣). If the particular machine pays a big bonus for a sequential royal flush, you would also want to see if the queen is in the center position and the jack adjacent to make a sequential royal possible.

The hands on the strategy card are ordered according to Expected Value in descending order. You simply look in the hand rank table to see which combination appears first, and you hold the cards for that draw. Within a half hour of play you will memorize most of the decisions without thinking about it. (Expected Value is explained in the chapter "What Does Expected Value Really Mean?" and on the supplement sheet that comes with the cue cards.)

Q. Are cue cards hard to use?

A. Abbreviations are necessarily used to make the cards pocket-sized, but the cards come with a detailed sheet that tells how to read the tables. You will quickly be able to identify any hand in the table. All serious players use hand rank tables, but if that seems too difficult then stick with the Precision Play method.

Q. Why don't you develop Precision Play rules for the cue cards instead of hand rank tables?

A. Some games are too complex to reduce the strategy to a set of rules without either a significant loss of accuracy or very complicated rules. A prime example is Double Bonus Poker.

Q. How can I be sure that a game's payback is as you state? Can't the machines be set for any payback the casino wants?

A. You're very astute. A video game is actually a special purpose digital computer, and a computer can be made to do whatever the programmer desires. Your protection is the Nevada gaming regulations which require that any machine representing a card game must be completely random, and every unseen card must have the same probability of appearing at any time. Since the Nevada Gaming Control Board tests each game before it can be used in Nevada, and it continues to spot check the machines even after they're installed, we are confident that the games obey the laws of probability close enough for our analyses to be accurate and useful. Also, the experience of many pros over years of play in the casinos supports this conclusion.

Q. Okay, but what about machines in other states?

A. It is our understanding that Nevada Gaming Control requires that any manufacturer selling gaming devices in Nevada must certify that all of their machines shipped anywhere meet the Nevada standards. Of course this doesn't prevent someone from changing the program chip after a machine leaves Nevada, but we have had only one report of a machine that didn't appear to be random, and that was a foreign made machine in an Indian casino on the east coast. To be safe, you may want to avoid games in unregulated areas (including cruise ships), especially if you don't recognize the machine manufacturer.

Q. Does the payoff schedule really matter? We have heard that a machine with lower payoffs will hit more often and thus generate about the same payback as a machine with the "full-pay" schedule.

A. This is simply not true, and it would be a gross violation of Nevada Gaming Regulations if it were. Since the games are required to be random, their payback is determined by the payoff schedule and your skill, not by the internal programming.

Q. Will I automatically get a game's rated payback?

A. This is the flip side of the preceding question. Some people seem to think that the machines are programmed to yield a predetermined payback regardless of how they play. Actually, the games are random, and the long-term payback is determined only by the payoff schedule and how you select discards. Since just a few seemingly minor playing errors can significantly reduce the payback, just sitting down at a full-pay machine will be of little value unless you learn an accurate strategy.

With Precision Play, however, it's never been easier. After just a few practice sessions you can cut the house percentage to a fraction of what you may now be giving up, and on the recommended games you can turn the odds in your favor.

Viewed another way, it's actually *fortunate* that the machines don't automatically give the rated payback. If they did, then everyone would get that payback, so no games offering over 100% potential payback would be made available by the casinos. The good games can exist only because most players make many errors, thus giving up an average of two to four percent of the potential payback. You get as close as desired to the rated payback because you learn the correct strategy. Winning opportunities are possible only because skill is involved in achieving maximum payback.

Q. Is it possible to get that "rated" payback?

A. Several commercial software packages are available that will quickly analyze a hand and indicate the best way to play. If it were allowed, you theoretically could achieve the game's rated maximum payback by taking a notebook computer to the casino and analyzing each dealt hand before selecting your hold cards. Don't be concerned that neither the casino nor Nevada regulations allow use of a computer while playing. The cost of slower play would be much greater than the cost of small errors in close decisions, so you are actually better off learning a "near perfect" strategy than trying to be perfect (see "What Does 'Optimum Play' Really Mean?" on page 29 for further discussion on this).

For most of the attractive games, any practical playing strategy can only approach the rated payback, and Precision Play closely approaches that limit with minimal memorization. More importantly, due to increased playing speed and reduced errors, Precision Play will yield a higher per-hour win rate than other strategies for most players.

Q. How can I tell if a machine is due to hit?

A. Many people have the mistaken belief that the machines are programmed to deal certain hands at a predetermined frequency or to "catch up" by paying a jackpot if it has gone a long time without any big payoffs. They often watch for someone walking away from a machine after putting in lots of money without a significant payoff, then proceed to pour their own money in, expecting it to hit a big pay very soon. You frequently hear about someone doing just that and quickly hitting a jackpot. Most such stories are fiction, and even when true they have no bearing on the future.

Some compulsive gamblers will stay at the same machine for hours or even days, putting in much more money than would be recovered even by hitting its biggest jackpot. They eventually leave only because they can't get any more money from the ATM or borrow any more money on their credit cards or from friends, yet they're convinced that "It's about to hit — I *know* it!" Sometimes they are then replaced by another compulsive gambler who repeats this strange performance.

So can a machine be due to hit? The answer is a resounding *NO!* It doesn't matter how long since a machine has paid a jackpot, a machine is *never* "due to hit." Neither is it any *less* likely to hit just after paying a jackpot. The chance of a jackpot on the next play is the same as it was yesterday or will be next week, even if the last play yielded a jackpot. Each outcome is determined randomly and is independent of history.

Q. But isn't timing important?

A. On some machines, the quality of cards received sometimes seems to be affected by how quickly we start the next play. Some background information may shed light on this. I have been told by a major manufacturer's field service technician that the random number generator programmed into the machine's computer starts "shuffling" the deck when a play is finished and any payout completed. It continues to do this until a player drops the first coin or presses one of the bet buttons.

Shuffling stops at that point so that the outcome can not be affected by the number of coins played. Thus, a quick replay gives the random number generator very little time to shuffle, and a long pause allows the deck to be shuffled perhaps thousands or millions of times. The idea is that the cards may be more truly random after a long pause.

But just how quickly can you make that next play? Computers are very fast. Even on the ten-year old technology in many machines, the deck may be shuffled many times in just a fraction of a second, so your pause or quick play probably has very little affect on the randomness of the game.

Clearly, timing does determine whether the next play will be a winner or a loser, but that has nothing to do with jumping on a machine because the previous player didn't win. The timing involved is a matter of milliseconds (thousandths of a second). If you had dropped that first coin or pressed the bet button a fraction of a second earlier or later, the outcome would have been completely different, and there is no way for you to know when would be the best time to press the button.

Q. Do the machines run in cycles?

A. Short cycles, consisting of several payoffs in a row, followed by several plays with no payoff, are quite common, especially on wild-card games. Some players claim that it is possible to take advantage of this by playing quickly after making a small payoff or catching a wild card on the draw, or pausing before the next play if there was no such occurrence, but this is highly speculative. All of the pros I know simply play as fast as they are able to play accurately, figuring that lost time is lost money.

Q. Will new varieties of video poker continue to emerge?

A. Of course they will. Each manufacturer is striving to sell more machines to the casinos, and each casino wants new games that will attract players away from the competition. In many cases it's not even necessary to replace the machine; just change the program chip and the artwork glass on the front panels, and voila — a "new" machine. Of course in most jurisdictions such a change must be approved and monitored by the gaming regulators.

Games with adjectives like "bonus," "double double," "triple," "plus" or "deluxe" in the name apparently fool many people into thinking they're getting a better deal when in fact they're not. Even if the "bonus" is real, it usually requires changes in playing strategy to take advantage of it. The moral is to generally avoid new games until they have been analyzed. (We do it regularly in *Video Poker Times*).

Q. I have a question that hasn't been answered here. Who can I ask?

A. E-mail your questions to *vptimes@lvcm.com*. If you're not "on line" you can send your questions by snailmail to the address in Appendix E on page 180, but please enclose a self-addressed, stamped envelope for a reply.

Appendix A

The ranking of hands for standard Jacks-or-Better Draw Poker is basically the same as for live table poker. In the quest to create new games, however, many newly contrived hand types have been defined. If you are familiar with poker hands, you will recognize the standard ones below, but some of the others may surprise you even if you are already familiar with video poker.

Since most of the "new" hand types are at the high end of the payoff schedule, I will start at the low end with the most frequently occurring final hands. Although an example is given for each hand type, these example hands are by no means definitive. There may be anywhere from one to over a million possible hands of each type. Remember also that except for a few special cases the cards may be in any order without affecting the hand's value.

The poker hands shown for each hand type below are only examples, and by no means should they be considered to be exhaustive. Also, except as specified for certain hands, the order of the cards has no bearing on the value of the hand. In these hands, "2W" means a wild deuce (the suit of a wild card is immaterial).

No Pair. No two cards of the same rank, and not all in sequence or of the same suit. Such a hand is usually a "zilch" hand (no payoff). The only video poker game I know of that may sometimes make a payoff for such a hand is Texas Hold'em.

6♦ J♣ 4♥ Q♠ 9♦

In a wild card game, it is not possible to have a wild card and not have a pair, but even so it may not be a winning hand.

6♦ 2W 7♥ K♠ A♣

One Pair. Two cards of the same rank, and three unrelated cards. Standard "Draw Poker" and certain variations require that the pair be jacks or higher for a payoff, although some games pay on a lower pair, and some require kings or better.

7♠ Q♠ 3♣ Q♥ K♦

A wild card will act as a match with the highest rank card to form a pair as in this hand.

9♣ 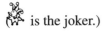 5♦ A♦ Q♠

 is the joker.)

Although some Joker Wild games return your bet on a pair of kings or aces, most wild card games do not pay on any one-pair hand.

Two Pair. Two cards of the same rank, two cards of another rank, and one unrelated card.

9♥ K♣ 9♠ 5♥ 5♦

This is the lowest actual winning hand in standard "Draw Poker" since a pair of jacks or better only returns your bet and thus is actually a push. Many wild card games do not pay on a two-pair hand. Two pair is not possible with a wild card in the hand since the wild card would automatically match with the pair to make three-of-a-kind.

Three-of-a-Kind. Three cards of the same rank, and two unrelated cards.

J♣ J♦ K♠ J♥ 3♦

Although three-of-a-kind is a decent winning hand in most games, it is generally the lowest payback hand (and only a push at that) in Deuces Wild and other games with four or more wild cards. A wild card automatically matches with any pair, so the following hand would also be three of a kind.

4♥ 2W A♠ 4♠ 8♣

Straight. Five cards in sequence, but not all the same suit. Note that the cards may appear in any order as long as they are of sequential ranks.

8♥ 10♠ Q♣ J♦ 9♥

Although an ace is usually considered to be a high card, it can also be used at the low end of a straight.

4♣ 3♥ 5♦ A♦ 2♠

In a wild card game, any wild card will automatically substitute for any missing card in the sequence.

7♦ 9♥ 🃏 8♥ 5♠

Flush. Any five cards of the same suit, but not in sequence.

Q♥ 4♥ A♥ 8♥ 7♥

In a wild-card game, any wild card automatically acts as whatever card will make the highest payoff with the other cards. In the following hand, the wild deuces act as spades, but it doesn't matter what rank spades are represented by the wild cards since a straight flush is not possible.

2W K♠ 8♠ 2W J♠

Full House. Three cards of the same rank, and two cards of another rank.

J♣ J♠ 5♦ J♦ 5♥

Note that a full house with wild cards can occur only with two pairs and a single wild card.

A♦ 2W 7♥ 7♠ A♣

Four-of-a-Kind. Four cards of the same rank, and one unrelated card, often called "quads" for short. In some games, different quads may have different payoffs.

10♦ 10♠ 10♣ Q♥ 10♥

In a wild card game, any wild card acts as a matching rank.

2W 8♦ 6♣ 2W 6♥

Four-of-a-Kind with Kicker. Four cards of a particular rank, and one card of another particular rank.

3♦ 3♠ 3♣ A♥ 3♥

You will find such a hand defined only in games such as Double Double Jackpot and Double Double Bonus Poker. It pays more than the same quads would pay without a specific fifth card.

Straight Flush. Five cards in sequence and suit. As for a straight, the cards may appear in any order as long as they are of sequential ranks, but they must all be of the same suit.

4♠ 5♠ 7♠ 3♠ 6♠

In a wild-card game, any wild card automatically acts as any missing card of the straight flush.

8♦ 🃏 10♦ 7♦ J♦

Five-of-a-Kind. Sometimes called "quints" for short, this obviously is possible only in a game with wild cards or in a game that is dealt from two or more decks. In a wild-card game it could consist of four-of-a-kind plus one wild card, three-of-a-kind and two wild cards, or a pair and three wild cards.

2W 6♠ 6♣ 2W 6♥

In a game such as Deuces Wild Bonus Poker, different five-of-a-kind hands may have different payoffs.

In Joker Wild, five-of-a-kind usually ranks higher than a wild royal.

9♦ 9♣ 🃏 9♥ 9♠

In a game dealt from multiple decks, five-of-a-kind could even look like this.

Q♦ Q♥ Q♦ Q♦ Q♥

Wild Royal. As with five-of-a-kind, a wild royal obviously is possible only in a game with wild cards. It could consist of four to the royal plus one wild card, three to the royal and two wild cards, or two to the royal and three wild cards. As for a straight flush, the cards may appear in any order.

K♣ 2W 2W Q ♣ 10 ♣

One high card and four deuces would not be considered a wild royal because it is worth more as four deuces (see below), but in

Deuces/Joker Wild it would be possible to make a wild royal with three deuces, the joker, and one high card. In some Joker Wild games, a wild royal is paid only as a straight flush.

Four Deuces. In Deuces Wild this is a secondary jackpot, paying anywhere from 1,000 to 3,000 coins depending upon the actual game type, or perhaps even more if it's a progressive.

2W 2W Q♠ 2W 2W

If you are dealt four deuces, I recommend holding all five cards to minimize the chances of making an error. However, some games pay more if the fifth card is an ace, in which case you would not hold the fifth card if dealt four deuces; you would draw, looking for an ace.

Royal Flush. An ace-high straight flush is called a royal flush. In most video poker games a royal flush with no wild cards is the biggest jackpot winner, paying 4,000 coins for five coins played. Some machines may pay 4,700 coins, 4,796 coins, or a progressive jackpot for a natural royal. As for a straight flush, the cards may appear in any order.

J♣ K♣ A♣ 10♣ Q♣

Wild cards do not apply since a royal flush with wild cards is a much lower ranked hand (see above). See also the Sequential Royal Flush below.

Five Wilds. Five wild cards are possible only in a game such as Deuces/Joker Wild. There is only one such hand possible compared to four natural royal flushes, so this may pay the biggest jackpot.

2W ❄ 2W 2W 2W

Sequential Royal Flush. A natural royal flush in which the cards happen to be in perfect ascending or descending order. On most machines, being in sequence does not affect the payoff, but on others such a hand may pay anywhere from ten to 25 times as much as it does when the cards are not in sequential order. Only a few casinos offer such a jackpot, and not on all games.

10♠ J♠ Q♠ K♠ A♠

In some cases, the sequence must be exactly as shown (especially if it is a progressive jackpot), but in most cases it may be in sequence in either direction. Again, wild cards to not apply since any royal flush with wild cards is a much lower ranked hand.

Five of a Kind (suited). Possible only in a game dealt from five decks instead of one. There are only 52 such hands possible compared to 480 possible royal flush hands in such a game.

6♣ 6♣ 6♣ 6♣ 6♣

In Five Deck Poker any suited quints wins the top payoff since there is no linked progressive jackpot, but in Five Deck Frenzy the next hand gets the glory.

Five Aces of Spades. Possible only in a game such as Five Deck Frenzy. There is only one such hand possible compared to 480 possible natural royal flushes, so this hand pays a big progressive jackpot.

A♠ A♠ A♠ A♠ A♠

In the quest for new games, it is likely that other artificial poker hands will be defined in the future. In any case, the payoff for each type of hand is typically inversely related to its probability of occurrence. This is why five-of-a-kind ranks higher than a wild royal flush in Joker Wild but lower in Deuces Wild.

Appendix B

This section includes all of the tables and charts referenced in the text. Here is a list of the tables:

Table 1: Progressive Jackpot Necessary for 100% to 105% Payback

Game	Bet	*	Jackpot necessary for long-term payback to be: 100%	102%	105%
5¢ Jacks-or-Better (7/5)	50¢	a	$1,180	$1,580	$2,185
25¢ Jacks-or-Better (8/5)	$1.25	b	$2,370	$3,375	$4,880
25¢ Jacks-or-Better (9/6)	$1.25	c	$1,250	$2,255	$3,760
25¢ 4-coin J-or-B (9/6)	$1.00	d	$1,000	$1,805	$3,010
25¢ Jacks-or-Better (10/6)	$1.25	e	$675	$1,675	$3,180
25¢ Jacks-or-Better (9/7)	$1.25	e	$710	$1,710	$3,220
25¢ Joker Wild (Kings)	$1.25	f	$780	$1,770	$3,250
25¢ Deuces Wild	$1.25	g	$620	$1,790	$3,540

* Notes:

a.   Perhaps the only 7/5 Jacks-or-Better that's likely to reach a high enough jackpot to exceed 100% payback. It's not recommended.

b.   On a $1 machine, the required jackpot is four times the amount shown for 25¢ machines with the same payoff schedule.

c.   The "full pay" machine with a large progressive jackpot is rare, but a nonprogressive 9/6 machine with a 4,700- or 4,796-coin jackpot yields nearly 99.9% long-term payback without the hassle of a tax report. Even better, a 9/6 that pays double on four sevens yields 100%, while the $1,000 jackpot with triple pay on four sevens yields 100.45%.

d.   The 9/6 four-coin Jacks-or-Better offers 100% payback even with a fixed $1,000 jackpot.

e.   I don't know of any progressives with these pay schedules, but the Stratosphere's 10/6 and 9/7 Jacks-or-Better offer over 100.6% payback even with a fixed $1,000 jackpot.

f.   I don't know of any progressives with these pay schedules, but the full-pay Joker Wild (Kings-or-Better) offers over 100.6% payback with a fixed $1,000 jackpot. I have also seen this game with a 4,700-coin royal.

g.   Deuces Wild, with its 100.75% long-term payback, is perhaps your best choice of commonly available machines where none of the higher paying Jacks-or-Better are available — provided you have a bankroll that can tolerate the larger fluctuations.

This page is applicable only to machines with a single progressive jackpot on the royal flush. See the "Payoff Schedule" chapters for full definitions of the referenced games; also "Multiple Progressives" and "Progressive Quads" for determination of when other types of machines will exceed 100% payback.

Abbreviations Used In Hand Rank Tables

If you have not used a hand rank table before, they may seem somewhat cryptic at first. A shorthand notation is necessary to keep the strategy tables compact and readable, and they are easy to follow once you understand these abbreviations:

RF	Royal Flush
SF	Straight Flush
2	Two cards to designated hand
3	Three cards to designated hand
4	Four cards to designated hand
i	Inside draw
di	Double Inside Draw
ti	Triple Inside Draw
>6	Top straight flush card must be 7 or higher
h0	No high cards[1]
h1	One high card
h2	Two high cards
h3	Three high cards
h4	Four high cards

These notations are combined to spell out a pre-draw hand. For example, **SF 3 di h1** would mean "three cards to a straight flush with a double inside draw, and it includes one high card." In Jacks-or-Better, Q♣-9♣-8♣-5♦-4♥ and J♣-9♣-7♣-8♣-3♣ are two examples of such a hand. In the second example, the J-9-7 of clubs makes a three-card straight flush with two inside cards missing (the ten and the eight). It includes one high card (the Jack). There are at least two other possible ways to play that hand. Holding J♣-9♣-7♣-8♦ it's a **Straight 4 i h1** (missing a ten), or holding J♣-9♣-7♣-4♣ it's a **Flush 4 h1**.

To achieve maximum payback, you should always draw to the combination that appears first in the hand rank table. For example, if J♣-9♣-7♣-8♦-3♣ were dealt in standard Jacks-or-Better you would find that **Flush 4** appears ahead of both **SF3 di** and **One high card**, so the four clubs should be held. **Straight 4 i** doesn't even appear except with an h3 notation, and this example contains only one high card. (If there is no "h" notation, then the number of high cards does not affect the decision.)

---

[1]What constitutes a high card depends upon the game. It might be a ten, jack, queen or king. An ace is always a high card, but note that high cards are not significant in most wild card games other than Joker Wild (Kings-or-Better).

Table 2: Pre-Draw Hands—Jacks-or-Better

For the standard full-pay game as defined in "The Payoff Schedule — Jacks-or-Better"

Predraw hand type	Notes	Number of occurrences	EV	Total Payback
Royal Flush	a	4	800.000	3,200
Straight Flush		36	50.000	1,800
4-of-a-Kind	b	624	25.000	15,600
Royal Flush 4	c	936	18.704	17,507
Full House		3,744	9.000	33,696
Flush		4,952	6.000	29,712
Three-of-a-Kind	d	54,912	4.303	236,286
Straight		10,128	4.000	40,512
Straight Flush 4	e	1,056	3.556	3,755
Two Pair		123,552	2.596	320,741
Straight Flush 4 i	f	4,032	2.375	9,576
High Pair	d	337,464	1.537	518,682
Royal Flush 3	g	28,356	1.401	39,727
Flush 4		85,512	1.188	101,588
K-Q-J-10 (unsuited)		5,964	.872	5,201
Low Pair	d	733,140	.824	604,107
Q-J-10-9 (unsuited)		6,360	.809	5,145
J-10-9-8 (unsuited)		6,648	.745	4,953
Q-J-9 suited		1,296	.731	947
J-10-9 suited		1,008	.728	734
Straight 4 h0	h	40,320	.681	27,458
Straight Flush 3 di h2	i	4,680	.639	2,991
Straight Flush 3 i h1		3,780	.632	2,389
Straight Flush 3 h0		6,048	.625	3,780
A-K-Q-J (unsuited)	j	5,664	.596	3,376
K-Q, K-J or Q-J suited		78,204	.591	46,716
A-K, A-Q or A-J suited		87,816	.578	50,758
Straight Flush 3 di h1	k	8,892	.538	4,784
K-Q-J-9 or A-h-h-10 (unsuited)	j	11,208	.532	5,963
Straight Flush 3 i h0		15,564	.531	8,264
K-Q-J (unsuited)		8,040	.515	4,141
Two high cards (unsuited)	l	391,116	.487	190,473
K-10,Q-10,J-10 suited	m	30,072	.477	14,344
One high card		406,704	.476	193,591
Straight Flush 3 di h0		6,768	.439	2,971
Zilch	n	84,360	.359	30,285
Totals		2,598,960		2,586,485
Long-Term Payback	p		99.54%	

Notes

These notes apply directly to the referenced hand types in Table 2, but many of the comments are also applicable to Tables 3 and 4.

a The 800-for-1 payback is applicable to the 4,000-for-5 jackpot for a royal flush. The payoff would be 940 if the jackpot pays 4,700-for-5 (increasing the total payback by .022%), 1,000 on a 4,000-for-4 machine (increasing the payback by .031%), or variable on a progressive jackpot.

b Hold all five cards when dealt four-of-a-kind. I've heard of cases where a machine malfunctioned and dealt a fifth card of the same rank, and the payoff was voided!

c A number following the hand description, such as "4" in this case, indicates the number of cards being held.

d Never hold a "kicker" with three-of-a-kind or a pair. This reduces the chances of catching another card of that rank, with an accompanying reduction in the Average Payback. Note that the rank of a second pair doesn't affect the payoff, so an ace is no better than any other card anyway.

e Four cards in sequence (no gaps) and of the same suit.

f An "i" following the number of cards being held indicates an inside draw (e.g., 7-8-9-J, needing a ten to fill the "inside" straight).

g Any royal flush draw is effectively an inside draw (with the exception of 10-J-Q-K, which is also a straight flush draw) so I don't bother differentiating between inside and open-end draws.

h The letter "h" indicates any high card (ace, king, queen or jack). "h0" means no high cards, "h1" means one high card, etc., included in the cards being held.

i The letter combination "di" indicates a double inside draw (e.g., 5-8-9 or 5-7-9, requiring two specific cards to complete the straight).

j These are the only playable inside straight draws. Draw to A-K-Q-J only if the Q-J are unsuited. Draw to the others only if no two of the high cards are suited.

k Includes suited A-2-3, A-3-4, etc., because two specific cards are required to complete the straight flush.

l Discard the ace from A-h-h unless it is suited with one of the other high cards, in which case discard the unsuited card. (See note h above.)

m Don't hold a suited 10 with an ace if the jackpot is less than 940-for-1, and don't hold a suited 10 with either an ace or a king if any discard is the same suit or is a ten or higher.

n "Zilch" means "nothing." When none of the described hands is dealt then all five cards must be discarded. This happens only about one hand in thirty.

p The Total Payback for each predraw hand is the product of its number of occurrences and its Average Payback. The approximate long-term payback for the game was calculated by summing the Total Payback column and dividing by the total number of possible pre-draw hands.

Table 3: Pre-Draw Hands—Deuces Wild

For the standard full-pay game as defined in "The Payoff Schedule – Deuces Wild"

#d	Hand type	EV	#d	Hand type	EV
4	Four deuces	200.000	0	Royal Flush (natural)	800.000
3	Royal Flush (wild)	25.000	0	Royal Flush 4	19.611
3	5-of-a-Kind (10-A) ①	15.000	0	Straight Flush	9.000
3	Deuces alone ②	15.026	0	4-of-a-Kind	5.851
2	Royal Flush (wild)	25.000	0	Full House	3.000
2	5-of-a-Kind	15.000	0	3-of-a-Kind	2.018
2	Straight Flush	9.000	0	Flush	2.000
2	4-of-a-Kind	5.851	0	Straight	2.000
2	Royal Flush 4	4.606	0	Straight Flush 4 ③	1.660
2	Straight Flush 4 ③	3.340	0	Royal Flush 3 (Q-high)	1.444
2	Deuces alone	3.260	0	Straight Flush 4 i ③	1.383
1	Royal Flush (wild)	25.000	0	Royal Flush 3 (others)	1.320
1	5-of-a-Kind	15.000	0	A-3-4-5 suited	1.106
1	Straight Flush	9.000	0	One pair ⑦	0.561
1	4-of-a-Kind	5.851	0	Flush 4	0.511
1	Royal Flush 4	3.524	0	Straight 4	0.511
1	Full House	3.000	0	Straight Flush 3 ③	0.510
1	Straight Flush 4 ③	2.233	0	Straight Flush 3 i ③⑧	0.430
1	3-of-a-Kind	2.018	0	J-10 suited	0.362
1	Flush	2.000	0	Straight Flush 3 di ③⑨	0.355
1	Straight	2.000	0	Straight 4 I	0.340
1	Straight Flush 4 i ③④	1.979	0	Q-J, Q-10 suited	0.332
1	Straight Flush 4 di ③⑤	1.702	0	K-Q, K-J, K-10 suited ⑩	0.327
1	Straight Flush 4i ace low	1.426	0	Zilch	0.322
1	Royal Flush 3 ⑥	1.127			
1	Straight Flush 3 ③	1.091			
1	Deuce alone	1.029		#d = Number of deuces	

Notes

① Do not break five-of-a-kind tens through aces to draw to the three deuces alone. The loss of those two high cards reduces the wild royal possibilities, lowering the EV to 14.94. On the other hand, discarding two low cards, whether it made five-of-a-kind or not, raises the EV to about 15.06.

② The EV shown for three deuces is the average for all cases that do not start out as five-of-a-kind or a wild royal. There are only three unique discard combinations: two low cards of different ranks, two unsuited honors of different ranks, or one honor and one low card. (An "honor" is any A, K, Q, J or 10.)

③ Except for special cases (notes 4, 5, 8 and 9 below) and 3-4-5-6 suited (no deuce), the top card for any straight flush draw must be seven or higher.

④ Includes 4-5-6 suited, plus one deuce.

⑤ Includes 3-4-5, 3-4-6 and 3-5-6 suited, plus one deuce.

⑥ J-, Q- or K-high only. (There are some Ace-high RF3s that are playable, but they are tricky to define, and the potential gain is very small.

⑦ Never draw to two pair. The EV when drawing to one pair is actually higher when a second pair is discarded than when three irrelevant cards are discarded. When dealt two pairs, it makes no difference which pair is held. (There is a comment on this situation in the Subjective Observations chapter.)

⑧ Includes 3-4-5 and 4-5-6 suited.

⑨ Includes 3-4-6 and 3-5-6 suited.

⑩ Only if no discard is of the same suit or higher than an eight.

Table 4: Pre-Draw Hands—Joker Wild (Kings-or-Better)

For the standard full-pay game as defined in "The Payoff Schedule – Joker Wild"

Hands *without* Joker		Hands *with* Joker	
Hand Type	**EV**	**Hand Type**	**EV**
Royal Flush	800.000	Five-of-a-Kind	200.000
Straight Flush	50.000	Wild Royal Flush	100.000
4-of-a-Kind	23.750	Straight Flush	50.000
Royal Flush 4	19.871	Four-of-a-Kind	23.750
Full House	7.000	Full House	7.000
Flush	5.000	Royal Flush 4	6.47
Straight Flush 4	4.236	Straight Flush 4	5.92
3-of-a-Kind	3.936	Flush	5.000
Straight Flush 4 I	3.118	Straight Flush 4 I	4.90
Straight	3.000	Straight Flush 4 di h1 ③	4.13
Two Pair	1.625	Three-of-a-Kind	3.936
Royal Flush 3	1.45	Straight Flush 4 di	3.79
High Pair	1.400	Straight	3.000
Flush 4	1.065	Flush 4 h1 or h2	1.98
Straight Flush 3	.740	Royal Flush 3	1.96
Low Pair	.731	Straight Flush 3	1.89
K-Q-J-10	.625	K-9 or A-5 suited+joker	1.81
Straight Flush 3 I	.61	Ace or King+joker	1.71
Straight Flush 3 di h1	.60	Straight Flush 3 I	1.70
A-K suited	.573	Straight Flush 3 di	1.57
Straight 4 h0	.562	Straight 4 h0	1.52
Straight Flush 3 di h0	.49	Flush 4 h0	1.52
K-Q, K-J or K-10 suited	.47	One mid card + Joker	1.47
Ace or King ①	.46	Joker alone	1.425
A-Q, A-J or A-10 suited ②	.453		
A-K (not suited) ①	.451		
Q-J, Q-10 or J-10 suited	.353	In this game, "h" means an ace or	
Zilch	.330	king only.	

Notes

①   Don't break up A-K to draw to just one of them; the Average Payback is reduced to .441 by the loss of a high card.

②   Don't break up A-Q, A-J or A-10 suited to draw to the ace alone unless there is another suited discard. (Loss of the suited high card reduces the EV of the ace alone to about .448, but loss of a suited card reduces the EV of the ace-high RF2 to about .442.)

③   King high or Ace low.

Table 5: Pre-Draw Hands—Bonus Deuces
(Also Bonus Sevens, but see note below)

#d	Hand type	EV	#d	Hand type	EV
4	Four deuces	400.000	0	Royal Flush (natural)	800.000
3	Deuces alone ①	22.414	0	Royal Flush 4	19.332
2	Royal Flush (wild)	20.000	0	Straight Flush	10.000
2	5-of-a-Kind	10.000	0	4-of-a-Kind	4.511
2	Straight Flush	10.000	0	Full House	4.000
2	4-of-a-Kind	4.511	0	Flush	3.000
2	Royal Flush 4	4.069	0	Straight	2.000
2	deuces alone	3.510	0	Straight Flush 4	1.894
1	Royal Flush (wild)	20.000	0	3-of-a-Kind	1.833
1	5-of-a-Kind	10.000	0	Straight Flush 4 I	1.638
1	Straight Flush	10.000	0	Straight Flush 4i ace low	1.362
1	4-of-a-Kind	4.511	0	Royal Flush 3	1.318
1	Full House	4.000	0	Flush 4	0.766
1	Royal Flush 4	3.123	0	Two pair ②	0.681
1	Flush	3.000	0	Straight Flush 3	0.592
1	Straight Flush 4	2.464	0	One pair	0.540
1	Straight Flush 4 i	2.230	0	Straight 4	0.511
1	Straight	2.000	0	Straight Flush 3 i	0.510
1	Straight Flush 4 di	1.953	0	Straight Flush 3 di	0.424
1	3-of-a-Kind	1.833	0	K-Q — J-10 suited ③	0.351
1	Straight Flush 4i ace low	1.677	0	Straight 4 I	0.340
1	Royal Flush 3 not A-high	1.151	0	Zilch	0.323
1	Straight Flush 3	1.145			
1	deuce alone	1.044	#d = Number of deuces		

Notes

①   Note that the draw to three deuces is worth more than even a pat wild royal, so we always draw to the three bare deuces.

②   Another big difference between this and regular Deuces Wild. Due to a full house paying the same as 4-of-a-kind, we hold both pairs.

③   Hold any two suited honors except ace-high, but not king high if any discard is of the same suit or is higher than a nine.

For *Bonus Sevens*, substitute "sevens" anywhere "deuces" appears above, and remember that there is no such thing as a fully open-ended straight or straight flush draw when holding a seven. Don't hold those suited connectors with one seven, and don't draw to an inside straight missing the seven. All straight flush draws will have a slightly lower EV due to the reduced payoff on the straight flush, but draws that can lead to five-of-a-kind will have a slightly higher EV than shown. I haven't figured it exactly since the analysis programs don't handle sevens wild, but I estimate about .8% lower payback than Deuces Wild with the same payoff schedule.

Table 6: Bankroll Necessary to Hit a Jackpot

Type of machine	Wager	Approximate bankroll necessary for the chances of hitting a royal to be:				
		50%	75%	90%	95%	99%
5¢ Jacks-or-Better (7/5)	50¢	$820	$1,640	$2,720	$3,540	$5,430
5¢ Jacks-or-Better (9/6)	25¢	$175	$345	$575	$750	$1,150
25¢ Jacks-or-Better (8/5)	$1.25	$1,650	$3,290	$5,460	$7,100	$10,900
25¢ Jacks-or-Better (9/6)	$1.25	$866	$1,730	$2,880	$3,750	$5,760
25¢ 4-coin Jacks-or-Better (9/6)	$1.00	$695	$1,390	$2,300	$3,000	$4,610
25¢ Joker Wild (Kings)	$1.25	$540	$1,080	$1,800	$2,340	$3,600
5¢ Deuces Wild	25¢	$85	$170	$285	$370	$570
25¢ Deuces Wild	$1.25	$430	$860	$1,430	$1,860	$2,850
5¢ Deuces Wild *	25¢	$40	$80	$130	$170	$265
25¢ Deuces Wild *	$1.25	$200	$395	$660	$855	$1,320
25¢ Bonus Deuces *	$1.25	$340	$680	$1,130	$1,470	$2,250

*   A "Jackpot" in these cases is either a royal flush or four deuces.

For a $1 machine, multiply each dollar amount given for the 25¢ machines by four.

For a $5 machine, multiply each dollar amount given for the 25¢ machines by 20.

When selecting a machine, keep in mind that in this table smaller numbers are better because you get the same chance of hitting a jackpot with a smaller starting bankroll. Or, conversely, you get a better chance of hitting a jackpot with any given fixed starting bankroll.

Note that the necessary bankroll climbs much faster than the desired probability of hitting a jackpot. It would take an unlimited bankroll (and unlimited playing time) to approach 100% certainty of hitting a jackpot.

Even in the best case of full-pay Deuces Wild, a bankroll equal to the royal jackpot gives only about an 80% chance of hitting that jackpot. This same bankroll on a 6-coin Jacks-or-Better gives only a 60% chance of a royal flush, and on a 8/5 Jacks-or-Better we need more than triple the bankroll for even a 75% chance of a royal. Again I say, *Avoid those short-pay machines!* (Exceptions include Aces & Eights and the 5-coin 8/5 triple progressive with a high enough jackpot on quads, but in these cases we're more interested in quads than the royal. Most machines that appear to be short pay really are.)

If you want to determine bankroll requirements for some other situation, refer to the chapter "Determining Bankroll Requirements."

Table 7: Risk of Ruin for Deuces Wild by Simulation

BR	Max # Plays →	500	1000	2000	4000	8000	16000	32000
	Prob. Ruin percent →	72	83	89	93	95	96	96
25	Mean End BR →	26	27	29	31	32	34	41
	Mean # Plays →	270	375	510	675	910	1200	2080
	Prob. Ruin percent →	42	64	77	85	90	93	93
50	Mean End BR →	53	55	57	60	64	68	80
	Mean # Plays →	415	640	920	1270	1730	2330	4000
	Prob. Ruin percent →	5	27	53	70	80	86	86
100	Mean End BR →	104	107	111	117	124	132	157
	Mean # Plays →	495	915	1490	2260	3230	4310	7390
	Prob. Ruin percent →	0	1	13	37	58	74	74
200	Mean End BR →	204	208	215	226	242	260	299
	Mean # Plays →	500	1000	1940	3430	5450	7860	12750
	Prob. Ruin percent →			0	2	21	46	53
400	Mean End BR →			415	430	458	497	559
	Mean # Plays →			2000	3990	7490	12600	20700
	Prob. Ruin percent →				0	0	9	28
800	Mean End BR →				830	862	920	1020
	Mean # Plays →				4000	8000	15700	29100
	Prob. Ruin percent →						0	1
1600	Mean End BR →						1720	1850
	Mean # Plays →						16000	31900

This table shows the risk of ruin — that is, the probability of losing your entire starting bankroll. This table represents the results of a Monte Carlo simulation of over 1.3 billion hands, equivalent to more than a thousand years of full time human play. Each session begins with a bankroll consisting of BR betting units and runs until either that bankroll is lost or you have made the "Max # Plays" shown in the column heading. Each table entry shows the mean (average) results of 6,000 such playing sessions, rounded off for ease of use. The first line is the probability of ruin (percentage of times the entire starting bankroll was lost before making the limiting number of plays). The next line is the mean ending bankroll (average number of betting units remaining at the end of the session), and the third line is the mean number of plays (average of the actual number of hands played in each session).

You may want to relabel the table for easier use. For example, if you play 650 hands per hour then 500 plays represents 500 ÷ 650 x 60 = 46 minutes playing time, so you could label the columns .75, 1.5, 3, 6, 12, 24 and 48 hours. If you play 25¢ machines, label the rows $31, $62, $125, $250, $500, $1,000 and $2,000. If you play $1 machines, label the rows $125, $250, $500, ... $8000. Refer to the "Probability of Ruin" chapter for further discussion of this table.

Expected Hourly Win Rates

When considering an opportunity, serious players are concerned primarily about volatility and expected win rate. Volatility has been discussed in the text, and several aspects of it have been covered in the preceding tables. The expected win rate is the long-term average, after playing long enough to ride out the fluctuations, and it is simply your advantage multiplied by your playing speed and your wager; i.e.,

$$W = \frac{A \bullet S \bullet B}{100}$$

where:

W   is the expected long-term win rate in dollars per hour,

A   is your advantage over the game in percent,

S   is your playing speed in hands per hour, and

B   is your total bet (in dollars) on each hand.

It is necessary to divide by 100 to convert percentage to a decimal fraction. See the chapter "How Fast Do You Play?" if you don't already know your playing speed.

For example, if you are playing a five coin quarter Deuces Wild at seven hundred hands per hour, then

$$W = \frac{0.75 \bullet 700 \bullet \$1.25}{100} = \$6.56$$

You can do this calculation easily with a pocket calculator, or you can look it up in following table.

Table 8: Long term average win rate (dollars per hour) on a 5-coin 25¢ machine

	PLAYING SPEED (hands per hour)							
Advantage	300	400	500	600	700	800	900	1000
.05%	.19	.25	.31	.37	.44	.50	.56	.62
.1%	.37	.50	.62	.74	.87	1.00	1.12	1.25
.2%	.75	1.00	1.25	1.50	1.75	2.00	2.25	2.50
.3%	1.12	1.50	1.87	2.25	2.62	3.00	3.37	3.75
.4%	1.50	2.00	2.50	3.00	3.50	4.00	4.50	5.00
.5%	1.87	2.50	3.12	3.75	4.37	5.00	5.62	6.25
.6%	2.25	3.00	3.75	4.50	5.25	6.00	6.75	7.50
.7%	2.62	3.50	4.37	5.25	6.12	7.00	7.87	8.75
.8%	3.00	4.00	5.00	6.00	7.00	8.00	9.00	10.00
.9%	3.37	4.50	5.62	6.75	7.87	9.00	10.12	11.25
1.0%	3.75	5.00	6.25	7.50	8.75	10.00	11.25	12.50

The percentages and win rates may be added for advantages not shown in the table. For example, if you are playing standard Deuces Wild at 100.75% payback you should add the win rates for .7% and .05% advantage, so at 600 hands per hour your expected average long-term win rate would be $5.25 + $.37 = $5.62 per hour. Alternatively, you could interpolate between the win rates for .7% ($5.25) and .8% ($6) and come up with the same result.

Of course, any slot club rebate should be included in your advantage. For example, that same Deuces Wild game at a casino that pays a .2% cash rebate on the slot card gives an advantage of .75% + .2% = .95%, so at the same 600 hands per hour it would be worth $6.75 + $.37 = $7.12 per hour.

You can also interpolate between playing speeds. For example, if you are playing 850 hands per hour with a .6% advantage then your expected win rate is mid way between $6 and $6.75, or about $6.37 per hour.

For a dollar machine, multiply all dollar values by four. For example, if you are playing Double Bonus Poker at 100.15% payback, plus .4% slot club rebate, then your advantage is .55%. At 800 hands per hour on a $1 machine your expected average long term win rate would be: 4 x ($5 + $0.50) = $22 per hour.

For a $5 machine, multiply the dollar amounts by twenty. For a nickel machine, divide by five.

Table 9: Attractiveness Quotient of Selected Games

The chart on the next page gives the Volatility Index and Attractiveness Quotient of a variety of attractive and partially attractive video poker games. All figures assume optimum play following an accurate hand rank table. Refer to the respective sections in this book for the definitions of Volatility Index (VI) and Attractiveness Quotient (AQ).

The second AQ column is for the same game played at the casino shown in the last column, including the slot club rebate or other bonus as indicated. The column headed "–2sd min." is another type of risk measurement, showing the greatest drawdown (number of bets lost) if you are unlucky enough to be two standard deviations below expectation, and the number of hands at which this minimum occurs.

Remember that the AQ is a relative figure, and it should be used only as a first guide in selecting a game. In many cases, comps are available on top of the cash rebates shown, which would further increase the attractivness of a game.

Game ①	Payback ②	VI	−2sd min. ③	AQ	AQ (including slot club, etc.)
Jacks-or-Better (8/5/4000) ④	97.27%	4.39	⑥	−621	−469 Treasure Island (.67%)
Bonus Poker (8/5/4000) ④	99.14	4.57	⑥	−187	−41 Treasure Island (.67%)
Jacks-or-Better (9/6/4000) ④	99.52	4.42	⑥	−108	43 Treasure Island (.67%)
Jacks-or-Better (9/6/4000) ④	100.42	5.09	8080 at 2530	↑	50 Fiesta (seq. royal)⑤
Jacks-or-Better (9/6/4700) ④	99.87	5.06	⑥	−25	24 Lady Luck (.25%)
Jacks-or-Better (10/6/4000) ④	100.67	4.44	2935 at 439	151	**173** Stratosphere (.1%)
Jacks-or-Better (9/7/4000) ④	100.78	4.16	2212 at 284	188	**212** Stratosphere (.1%)
Aces & Eights ($100 on 4 A,8)	100.15	4.67	9270 at 3570	32	139 Circus Circus (.5%)
All American Poker	100.70	5.18	3830 at 547	135	**232** Las Vegas Hilton (.5%)
Double Bonus Poker (10/7)	100.15	5.32	18800 at 12600	28	154 Treasure Island (.67%)
Double Double Bonus	98.8	5.53	⑥	−191	−151 Hypothetical .25%
Double Double Jackpot (10/6/5)	101.21	6.04	3010 at 249	**200**	Full pay extinct?
Double Double Jackpot (10/7/4)	100.96	5.84	3550 at 370	164	**199** Hypothetical .2%
Double Double Jackpot (9/6/5)	100.12	6.02	25900 at 18500	23	65 Horseshoe (.25%)
Flush Attack (unlinked)	101.8	5.49	1670 at 93	**328**	Full pay extinct?
Deuces Wild (15/9/4000)	100.75	5.08	3440 at 459	148	**180** Fiesta (seq. royal) ⑤
Deuces Wild (15/9/4700)	101.06	5.65	3010 at 284	188	196 Plaza dinner coupon
Bonus Deuces	100.93	7.10	4920 at 482	131	144 Sam's Town (.093%)
Loose Deuces (15/10)	100.95	8.38	4840 at 334	113	**173**
Joker Wild (Kings-or-Better)	100.63	5.12	4160 at 661	123	**180** Fiesta 4700-coin royal
Joker Wild (Two Pair) (5000)	102.00	5.34	1420 at 71	**376**	Full pay extinct?
Double Joker Wild (AC)	99.9		⑥	−90	**186** Bally's Park Place⑦

① Full pay version (defined elsewhere) except as indicated.

② Expected long-term payback when following an accurate hand rank table.

③ Number of bets lost at the minimum of the −2 standard deviation curve, and the number of hands (thousands) to that point.

④ Assumes unmodified Precision Play for the basic 9/6/4,000 Jacks-or-Better.

⑤ With payoff of 60,000 coins for a sequential royal in either direction.

⑥ The negative standard deviation curves will never flatten out or cross above zero if the game's payback does not exceed 100%.

⑦ For three-coin $1 game (100.39%), including .75% cash rebate (coupon mailed later for rebate).

The best opportunities are highlighted in bold print.

Good Games, and Where To Find Them

A t the time this book is being written, many casinos in Las Vegas and elsewhere are advertising their video poker with claims such as:

"It's true! We have more 25¢ video poker machines, paying back 100% or more, than any other casino in the city." [Perhaps, but they don't say *how much* over 100% or what percentage of their machines are over 100%. Also, this particular ad avoided comparison with casinos outside Las Vegas city limits.]

"Everybody's winning at …" [Of course! And I've got some prime Nevada ocean front property for sale.]

"Over 100% payback! It's certified. Nobody's better." [Yes, at this casino, the "certified" games do offer over 100% payback, and, in fact, a few are over 100.7%; but the last part, "Nobody's better," simply is not a valid claim since there are many better places in Las Vegas to play video poker. Also, one must wonder just who did the certification? A CPA? An advertising agent? It doesn't appear to have been any established video poker authority.]

"The Royal Flush Capital of the World." [Although this particular casino used to offer a variety of attractive video poker that might have justified this glorious self-proclaimed title, the offerings began going downhill a few months before this book went to press.]

"Hand for hand, nobody has more payouts ... Nobody!" [Perhaps, but that has absolutely no direct bearing on a game's payback. In fact, it's more likely to have an *inverse* relationship. This claim is apparently justified by the only Sevens-or-Better game I've ever seen. Since there are four more "high" pairs that will return the player's bet, nearly 58% of all plays will yield a payout even though the maximum payback is only 99.047%.]

"More Royals Than Any Casino Anywhere!" [Nice try, but a subsequent ad by another local casino showed that this was simply not true. And that's not even considering a huge Connecticut casino which very likely pays more royal flushes even though there are no attractive games.]

"World's Loosest Video Poker." [This is the granddaddy of them all. Since Nevada regulations require the machines to be random, no machine can legally be "looser" than any other except by having a better payoff schedule. Casinos making such vague claims generally offer few if any really attractive games.]

While it's true that it's possible to be a long-term winner on certain machines in most of those casinos, these casinos are not necessarily the best places to play video poker. Remember, the number of payouts or royals is not by itself a reliable indicator of how good the video poker is at a given casino.

The predecessor of this book included a very detailed survey of attractive games in southern Nevada, along with a few comments about other areas. That was practical because it was printed in booklet form in small quantities and thus could be updated every few months. Such a survey in this book would quickly become outdated, so instead I offer a few guidelines about where you're likely to find the best games later in this Appendix.

What Games To Play?

There are several types of video poker games that offer over 100% long-term average payback. These include the full-pay Deuces Wild, Bonus Deuces, Loose Deuces and Joker Wild described in this book, as well as a Jacks-or-Better "Draw Poker that combines a full-pay schedule with a progressive jackpot or bonus payouts. (See the Payoff Schedule chapters for definitions of "full pay" for each of these types of machines.) Another very popular game that offers slightly over 100% payback is Double Bonus Poker, but its strategy is more complex. In Atlantic City there is currently a somewhat attractive version of Double Joker Wild. (See Appendix E on page 180 for cue cards for these and other attractive games.)

Until you advance to the more complex games, the only machines you should seriously consider are the basic games and their enhanced payback versions, such as:

- Any full-pay three- or four-coin machine, or any machine in which the basic full-pay schedule pushes the payback over 100%;

- Any machine that is full-pay and offers a meaningful added bonus (e.g., triple pay on four sevens);

- A progressive 2nd Chance machine; or

- Other such games when a progressive jackpot, slot club rebate, comps, and/or any other bonuses offered by the casino push the total payback significantly above 100%. (In some cases a slot club or promotion may turn an otherwise unattractive game into a very attractive situation.)

Other variations often seem to be attractive, but most reduce the payback significantly below 100%. Some may offer nearly the same total payback, but the bonus paid on certain infrequent hands must be offset by shorting other payoffs, usually the full house and flush (Jacks-or-Better) or quads (Deuces and Joker Wild). Because of the short pays on these more frequently occurring hands, bankroll fluctuations are increased, often with no offsetting advantage.

I can't say it too often; stick with the recommended games, and always play enough coins to qualify for the jackpot.

Where To Find The Good Games

As noted earlier, it is not practical to include a detailed survey in this book as I did in *Video Poker – Precision Play*. However, in Las Vegas, with its heavy concentration of video poker, there are several casinos that have had a history of offering good games. With rare exceptions, the best opportunities are not found on the main Strip. Check out the following area casinos (listed alphabetically):

Arizona Charlie's (Decatur Ave. near Charleston)
El Cortez (Downtown Las Vegas)*
Eldorado (Downtown Henderson)
Fiesta (Rancho Blvd., North Las Vegas)*
Orleans (Tropicana Road, west of the Strip)
Plaza (Downtown Las Vegas)*
Rainbow (Downtown Henderson)
Reserve (Lake Mead Drive at I-515 in Henderson)
Sam's Town (Boulder Highway at Flamingo)*
Santa Fe (Rancho Blvd. north at US 95)*
Skyline (Boulder Highway at Sunset Road in Henderson)*
Stratosphere (Far north end of the Strip)
Sunset Station (Sunset Road at I-515 in Henderson)

* The casinos flagged with an asterisk had the best games and/or promotions at the time this book is going to press, but that is no guarantee that they are still the best.

Also, if you happen to be around when a new casino opens, check it out immediately. No, this has nothing to do with the rumor that new machines pay off more often, but new casinos often unintentionally put in some high-paying games or offer special promotions that are soon changed or removed.

Several specific games are mentioned in the text. Again, there's no guarantee that these games are still where I found them, but they are unlikely to change soon because they have been in place for several years. Here's where I found them:

Deuces Wild, full pay 5¢: **Skyline, Fiesta, Reserve**
Deuces Wild, full pay 25¢ with 4700-coin royal: **Plaza, El Cortez**
Deuces Wild, full pay 25¢ with progressive royal or $15,000 sequential royal: **Fiesta, Santa Fe**
Jacks-or-Better, full pay 5¢ plus bonus: **Plaza, Fiesta**
Aces & Eights, 5¢ and 25¢: **Circus Circus**
Joker Wild, 25¢ with 4700-coin royal: **Arizona Charlie's, Fiesta, Railroad Pass, Santa Fe**
Joker Wild, near full pay 5¢ progressive: **Gold Spike**

Also, watch for seasonal promotions. Many casinos have specials to attract new customers, especially during slow times of the year. While it may not be true in other parts of the country, in Las Vegas, the outlying "locals" casinos often have the most favorable promotions, but they may not advertise them in the tourist magazines. Watch for ads in the local newspapers, especially on the weekend.

A subscription to the *Las Vegas Advisor* will yield a coupon booklet worth many times the subscription cost in video poker bonuses alone, plus it will notify you of many promotions, video poker and otherwise. More importantly, a subscription to *Video Poker Times* will keep you abreast of the latest and best in video poker and provide accurate strategies for new and attractive games.

You can also find some tips on my web site at:
http://www.vegasplayer.com/video-poker.html

Appendix D

Gaming Regulations & Enforcement

Several times in this book I have referred to the gaming regulations of Nevada and other jurisdictions. Following is the most pertinent section of the Regulations of the Nevada Gaming Commission and State Gaming Control Board, Carson City, Nevada, as Adopted July 1, 1959, and Current as of March, 1996. Since it was mailed to me directly from the State Gaming Control Board on December 20, 1997, I assume that it was still current as of that date.

14.040 Minimum standards for gaming devices. All gaming devices submitted for approval:

1. Must theoretically pay out a mathematically demonstrable percentage of all amounts wagered, which must not be less than 75% for each wager available for play on the device.

(a) Gaming devices that may be affected by player skill must meet this standard when using a method of play that will provide the greatest return to the player over a period of continuous play.

(b) The chairman may waive the 75% standard if the manufacturer can show to the chairman's satisfaction that this requirement inhibits design of the device or is inappropriate under the circumstances, the device theoretically pays out at least 75% of all wagers made when all wagers are played equally, and the device otherwise meets the standards of subsections 2 through 6. A waiver will be effective when the manufacturer receives written notification from the chairman that this standard will be waived pursuant to this paragraph. A waiver of this standard pursuant to this paragraph is not an approval of the device.

2. Must use a random selection process to determine the game outcome of each play of a game. The random selection process must meet 95% confidence limits using a standard chi-squared test for goodness of fit.

(a) Each possible permutation or combination of game elements which produce winning or losing game outcomes must be available for random selection at the initiation of each play.

(b) For gaming devices that are representative of live gambling games, the mathematical probability of a symbol or other element appearing in a game outcome must be equal to the mathematical probability of that symbol or element occurring in the live gambling game. For other gaming devices, the mathematical probability of a symbol appearing in a position in any game outcome must be constant.

(c) The selection process must not produce detectable patterns of game elements or detectable dependency upon any previous game outcome, the amount wagered, or upon the style or method of play.

3. Must display an accurate representation of the game outcome. After selection of the game outcome, the gaming device must not make a variable secondary decision which affects the result shown to the player.

4. Must display the rules of play and payoff schedule.

5. Must not automatically alter pay-tables or any function of the device based on internal computation of the hold percentage.

6. Must meet the technical standards adopted pursuant to section 14.050.

7. Except for devices granted a waiver pursuant to subsections 1(b), or 8, each gaming device exposed for play in the State of Nevada by any gaming licensee, including an operator of a slot machine route, must meet the standards and requirements set forth within subsection 1, as though the gaming device had been submitted for approval subsequent to September 28, 1989.

8. The chairman of the board or his designee may waive the requirements of subsection 7 for a licensee exposing a gaming device to the public for play, if the licensee can demonstrate to the chairman's satisfaction that:

(a) After the waiver the aggregate theoretical payout for all amounts wagered on all gaming devices exposed for play by the licensee at a single establishment meets the 75% standard of subsection 1, and

(b) The licensee is unable to bring the device into compliance with the requirements of subsection 1, because of excessive cost or the unavailability of parts.

(Adopted: 7/89. Amended: 9/89; 10/92. Effective: 1/1/93.)

The wording of paragraph 1(a) appears to make it legal for a game to pay back even less than 75% to an unskilled player. However, I have never seen or heard of a video poker game with a payback that was anywhere near that low.

Paragraph 2 is the most important to us. In essence, it tells us that video poker in Nevada must be an honest game. Since video poker is "representative of live gambling games" this regulation mandates that the probabilities must be very close to that of cards being dealt from a thoroughly shuffled standard deck of playing cards. (I say "very close" because the first part of Paragraph 2 says "The random selection process must meet 95% confidence limits using a standard chi-squared test for goodness of fit." This leaves room for the apparently nonrandom anomalies reported by some players and discussed in my new book *Video Poker Anomalies and Anecdotes*.) Therefore, unlike players of "no brainers" (reels slots) we don't have to be concerned about the low 75% minimum payback specified in paragraph 1; we can determine the maximum payback of most video poker games directly from the payoff schedule, and even most unskilled players are likely to get within a few percentage points of that figure.

But laws and regulations are of little value without enforcement. Here again, Nevada leads the way. Nevada Gaming Control has assured me that they do regular spot checks to ensure that the program chips in the machines match the approved chips. Also, I have been told that they will do a special check if you report a suspicious machine.

Unfortunately, such may not be the case in other jurisdictions. In 1996 I exchanged several letters with Mr. Seth H. Briliant, Senior Counsel, New Jersey Division of Gaming Enforcement. I repeatedly asked and rephrased the same questions; in my opinion, he repeatedly skirted the issues and avoided a straightforward answer. Finally, Mr. Briliant suggested I address any further correspondence to the bureau's supervisor, Mr. Richard Williamson. I did so and received a response not from Mr. Williamson but from New Jersey Deputy Attorney General Timothy C. Ficchi.

Mr. Ficchi did not quote any regulations but instead answered my concerns with the statement: "Your primary interest, as expressed in your letter, is the comparison between Nevada and New Jersey in the approval of video poker programs. Please be advised that although New Jersey does not have a regulation as explicit as Nevada's Section 14.040, the approvals for video poker machines in this jurisdiction are governed in a like manner." Mr. Ficchi's assurances did not give me much confidence about enforcement in the future.

My impression was that the New Jersey officials delighted in treating me as if I knew very little about gaming or video poker. These communications left me very unsatisfied until I read Steve Bourie's interview of Mr. Williamson in *American Casino Guide—1998*. They go about it in a different way, but it sounds like they are thorough.

In addition, I have received reports from many pros who have played in Atlantic City, and none has suggested that they had encountered what we would call "dishonest" video poker.

But at least New Jersey has regulation and enforcement. What concerns me more is the proliferation of legalized gambling on native American reservations where, in most cases, there is little or no meaningful regulation and no recourse for an outsider who thinks he has been cheated. So far problems have been rare, and I have received only one report of an apparently nonrandom video poker machine, but anything can happen as they expand.

Even worse are machines on cruise ships and in foreign countries. My best recommendation is to be cautious in any such jurisdiction, especially if a game's displayed rules or payoffs seem too good to be true.

Perhaps our best protection when playing video poker outside Nevada is the fact that Nevada is still the biggest market for gaming machines, so the major manufacturers strive to satisfy Nevada regulations.

Appendix E

Other Video Poker Products

Video Poker Times™

Edited and published by Dan Paymar.

Good opportunities come and go. Often a new game or promotion appears that is quickly analyzed by the pros who find out that it pays well over 100%. It is hit by dozens of skilled players who extract as much as possible before the casinos discovers that it is losing to the players, and soon it is gone.

Can you blame the casinos? Of course not. They have a right to expect a profit on anything they offer, but you have the right to be among those few who profit when such an opportunity arises. But how is that possible? You can keep up with the rapidly changing world of video poker by subscribing to *Video Poker Times*.

This newsletter has been published bimonthly since 1993. The data in its four to eight (usually six or more) 8.5 x 11 pages are invaluable to all players seeking a profit at video poker. Each issue includes at least one lead article of interest to serious players, often an optimum strategy for a new 100%-plus game. The Tidbits column (new opportunities) and Crier's Corner (lost opportunities) will keep you up to date. There's also a Question and Answer column and other valuable information.

A one year subscription to *Video Poker Times* (six issues) is $45 first class U.S. postage paid, but mention that you have this book and you can take a $5 discount. Back issues are available, and much of the material is collected in *The Best of Video Poker Times*. See the special combination offers below.

Individual back issues of *Video Poker Times* are also available. An index and price list are available from Dan on request by mail or e-mail.

Best of Video Poker Times™ (and more)

This 76-page book contains all of the best articles, tidbits, and other columns from *Video Poker Times* issues 1.1 (September/October, 1993) through 4.3 (May/June, 1996). Nothing of current value has been omitted, and several articles have been updated as appropriate. This book includes several video poker articles written for publication elsewhere.

It would cost over $100 to get all of this in the original publications, but it's all together here, updated to be current as of May, 1997, organized and conveniently indexed for only $19.95 plus shipping and handling.

The Best of Video Poker Times, Volume II

This 68-page book contains all the best articles and other columns from *Video Poker Times* issues 4.4 (July/August, 1996) through 7.2 (March/April, 1999). Nothing of current interest has been omitted. Conveniently organized and indexed for only $24.95 plus shipping and handling.

Video Poker Software

I am currently in the development stages of *Precision Video Poker*™, a software package for both the PC and Macintosh platforms that will encompass all of the best features of all currently available programs, plus much more.

As you can imagine, this is a big project. If you are an idea person or a programmer, and would like to be a part of this project, please contact me at *vptimes@lvcm.com* and let me know your skills and interests.

For reviews of software packages currently available, refer to issue 3.2 of *Video Poker Times*. This review is also reproduced in *The Best of Video Poker Times (and more)*. The best package at the time of that review was *Video Poker Tutor*, and version 2 is still one of the best.

Until *Precision Video Poker* is available, you can download a free version of *Dynamic Video Poker* for the Macintosh from my web site at http://www.vegasplayer.com/video-poker.html

Video Poker Anomalies & Anecdotes

This new booklet contains many amusing anecdotes, plus reports from readers of *Video Poker Times* about suspected anomalies in the machines. Although many players swear that the anomalies exist, we recommend reading this book for amusement only.

Video Poker Cue Cards

(You Can Take It With You)

Laminated, shirt pocket size cue cards have been developed for most of the attractive games. Each card provides an accurate hand rank table for one game, and in some cases one or more variations on that game.

Many professionals play with a cue card, so don't be embarrassed to use one.

All payback percentages shown below assume you've selected the game with the indicated payoff schedule and are playing it according to the strategy given on the card. Typically the quoted payback is about .02% to .05% below maximum payback as computed by game analysis software to allow for human error. If you're perfect, you can gain a bit more than the payback shown, but even if you're human like the rest of us you can easily have a significant edge over the house.

Note: Numbers such as "9/6" following a game name refer to the payoffs that are most frequently changed. For Jacks-or-Better they refer to the full house and flush, respectively; that is, 9/6 means the game pays 9-for-1 (45-for-5) for a full house and 6-for-1 (30-for-5) for a flush.

The cards come with a separate sheet that clarifies the abbreviations and notes. Cards are $4 each, or as low as $3 each for ten or more.

Currently available cards:

Jacks-or-Better. Accurate strategy for full-pay 9/6 (99.52%, or 99.85% with 4700-coin royal), short-pay but more commonly available 8/5 (97.3%), super-full-pay 10/6 (100.67% at Stratosphere), common 8/5 Bonus Poker (99.2%), Aces and Eights (100.15% + .5% slot club rebate at Circus Circus), Aces & Faces (99.24% plus .25% slot club rebate at Horseshoe) and most Jacks-or-Better progressives.

Jacks-or-Better (9/7) at 100.78% at Stratosphere. This variation requires a slightly modified strategy to get the most out of the game, although you will get 100.62% even if you use the 9/6 strategy above.

Double Bonus Poker at 100.15%. This game is widely available around southern Nevada. Add any slot club cash rebate (e.g., .5% at Las Vegas Hilton).

Double Double Jackpot 10/6/5 at 101.2% or 9/6/5 at 100.1%. This is one of the easiest games to play accurately. The 10/6/5 version may be extinct, but the 9/6/5 is plentiful in southern Nevada.

All American Poker at 100.7%. The accurate strategy for this often overlooked game. Occasionally available paying more than standard for quads (103%) on some Bally *GameMaker* machines. In many areas outside Nevada this is the only game available that offers over 100% payback. It has the advantage of almost matching the payback of Deuces Wild with lower volatility (smaller expected bankroll fluctuations) although the strategy is more complex than Deuces Wild.

Flush Attack at up to 101.8%. This is the optimum "Flush 50" strategy for unlinked machines that go into "Attack" mode after three flushes (look for **SHL WINNER** on the screen on all machines). As far as we know, most machines now take four flushes to trigger attack mode, but you can often pick up one or two "free" flushes from previous players, making this strategy viable.

Deuces Wild at 100.75% (101.05% with 4700-coin royal at Plaza). This is the most widely available game that is significantly over 100% payback. Strategy modifications for the $15,000 sequential royal flush at the Fiesta are included (.6% extremely long term added payback).

Bonus Deuces at 100.9% at Sam's Town (plus .093% slot club cash rebate and comps worth perhaps several times that).

Loose Deuces 15/10 at 100.95%. This card is also accurate for the more common 15/8 version (100.09%). The 17/10 version (101.6%) appears to be extinct, but the strategy is given in *Video Poker Times* issue 3.1 should you encounter one.

Deuces Deluxe at 100.4% (plus .4% slot club cash rebate at Stardust). This payoff schedule is also found on machines with different names at a few other casinos.

Joker Wild (Kings or Better) at 100.6%. This game appeared to be on the endangered list, but now it seems to be making a comeback at several casinos, some with 4700-coin royal which adds another .3%.

Joker Wild (Two Pair) at up to 102%, but full-pay machines are only sporadically available and seldom last long. Recommended only for someone who is always on the lookout for the best opportunities.

AC Double Joker Wild (Atlantic City) at up to 99.9%, or 100.3% in the three-coin version at one casino, but full-pay machines are scarce.

LV Double Joker Wild (Las Vegas) at up to 100.6% in (this pay schedule is not available in Atlantic City and is rare even in Las Vegas).

Ordering Information

Following is ordering information for my products, including some combination offers. All business is currently by mail only with check or money order. Additional copies of this book, as well as some of the items described in this and the next Appendix, are available direct from ConJelCo, in which case you can order by phone or e-mail and use your credit card.

Please write a letter indicating the quantity of each item you want or visit my web site for an order form. Make your check or money order payable to Dan Paymar, and send it to the address below. Except as noted for cue cards, all prices below include first class US or air mail postage.

Video Poker Times

One-year subscription (six issues). Specify starting issue (your subscription will start with the current issue if not specified).

U.S.: $45.00, Canada: $50.00, Other foreign: $60.00

The Best of Video Poker Times (and more)

See description earlier in this Appendix.

U.S.: $21.95 Canada: $24.00, Other foreign: $28.00

The Best of Video Poker Times, Volume II

See description earlier in this Appendix.

U.S.: $26.95 Canada: $29.00, Other foreign: $32.00

Combination 1

Both *Best* books plus one year of *Video Poker Times* starting with the current issue (or specify desired starting issue).

U.S.: $80.00, Canada: $85.00, Other foreign: $95.00

Combination 2

Both *Best* books plus three years of *Video Poker Times* starting with issue 7.3 (through issue 10.2).

U.S.: $130.00, Canada: $140.00, Other foreign: $150.00

Video Poker Anomalies & Anecdotes

See description earlier in this Appendix.

U.S.: $7.50, Canada : $8.50, Other foreign: $10.00

Video Poker Cue Cards

List the cards desired (see descriptions earlier in this Appendix). Pricing is as follows:

> Fewer than five (mix or match) at $4.00 each
> Any five or more (mix or match) at $3.50 each
> Any ten or more (mix or match) at $3.00 each

Shipping and handling on cue cards, add, per order: U.S.: $1.00, Canada: $2.00, Other foreign: $2.00 plus 10¢ per card. No additional S&H charge when combined with any other order.

Make your check or money order **payable to Dan Paymar** and send it to:

> Dan Paymar
> PMB 141
> 2540 S. Maryland Pkwy
> Las Vegas, NV 89109

Outside the U.S.

All payments must be in U.S. dollars by international money order or a check drawn on a U.S. bank for the amount shown above for your location. Shipment only to countries where declarations are not required.

For questions and comments only, send e-mail to Dan at:

> vptimes@lvcm.com

For the latest information and order form, visit my web site at:

> http://www.vegasplayer.com/video-poker.html

Recommended Reading

The following publications are unique for their accuracy and sound advice. Each of these books is worth many times its price for valuable information it contains. To reap maximum rewards from your play, use these books in conjunction with my publications.

Bargain City by Anthony Curtis. $11.95 from Huntington Press. Anthony was referring mostly to blackjack players when he said "A world-class card counter can win one bet an hour, at best. An amateur comp wizard can win one bet an hour standing on his or her head." However, most of his wisdom on "couponomy" applies equally to video poker and other games. Learn the art of utilizing coupons to their fullest and getting small to moderate comps in Las Vegas. Whatever stakes or games you play, this is a "must have." (But skip the video poker chapter — it's far too simplified.)

Guide to Slot Clubs by Jeffrey Compton. First edition $9.95 from Huntington Press. This book gives an interesting "Short History of Slot Clubs," then it asks and answers the important question, "Why Slot Clubs?" It then compares the various characteristics of slot clubs and offers guidelines on picking the best club for your particular needs. A chapter titled "The Benefits" tells how to receive the intangible benefits that most players don't even know are available. In some cases, the intangibles are much more valuable than the cash rebate or comps described in the club literature. The most useful section is the survey which gives a full page of information on nearly every slot club in the Las Vegas area. The author also offers his "Optimal Strategy," and much of the information is slanted to video poker players. This book provides a summary of information that can't be found together anywhere else. It is a must have for any slot or video player.

The Frugal Gambler by Jean Scott. $11.95 from Huntington Press. Her favorite word is "free." Jean and her husband Brad stay in Las Vegas hotels, sometimes for months at a time, spending little or no money of their own. Often, they fly to and from their home in the Midwest for free as well. Obviously they must be high rollers, making $1,000 bets on blackjack and craps. Right? Wrong! They are video poker players, and they play mostly quarters and sometimes dollars. So how do they get such great comps? Her techniques were the subject of a CBS 48 Hours TV show. In this book, Jean tells in great detail how she goes about getting almost unlimited comps while beating the casinos at their own game. This book works hand-in-hand with my publications and *Guide To Slot Clubs*.

American Casino Guide by Steve Bourie. $14.95 from Casino Vacations. This 450-page book, which is updated every year, is another "must have" for anyone who frequents casinos anywhere in the United States. Besides lots of good articles there are maps and data for nearly every casino in the country. In the back are over fifty coupons, any one of which may alone be worth the price of the book. Perhaps the most informative parts are a dialog with Nevada Gaming Control representatives about the honesty of slot machines, and a discussion with an IGT (International Game Technology) representative about the internal operation of video poker machines.

Comp City by Max Rubin. $39.95 from Huntington Press (hardcover only). If you play in Las Vegas with a gambling bankroll of $1,000 or more you would be crazy not to have this book. It's especially good if you're a blackjack player but not an expert card counter. This book shows how to get much more in comps than your expected loss. But don't get the idea that this book is for high rollers only; there's also lots of information that's useful to video poker and low stakes players.

How to Keep More of What You Win by Walter L. Lewis, CPA. $11.95 + $2.00 S&H from Impulse Publishing, c/o Kelly Simon Productions, 1600 Ranch Drive, Latrobe, PA 15650 or call 800-747-5599. This little 50-page book goes into quite some detail about keeping records and reporting your winnings and losses on your income tax return.

Card Player magazine, 3140 S. Polaris Ave., Ste. 8, Las Vegas, NV 89102 or call 702-871-1720. Published biweekly. Back issues are available at $3.95 each including postage. The current issue is free in many card rooms.

Some of the terms used in the text may be a little confusing because they have a special meaning as applied to video poker.

86   The act by a casino of barring a player, either from a particular game or from the entire casino. Such a person is said to have been "86'd." (In Nevada, and in many other jurisdictions, a casino has the status of a private club, so anyone's "membership" can be cancelled at any time for any reason, or with no reason given.) Barring of professional players has been a common problem for blackjack card counters, but it has been rare for video poker players.

Attractiveness Quotient

A relative measure of the general attractiveness of a game, particularly good for recreational players to compare games. See "The Attractiveness Quotient" on page 27 in the text for more information.

Cycle   The average number of hands per royal flush (or other top jackpot). Remember, however, that the games are random, so don't expect to get exactly one royal flush per "cycle," and don't get the idea that a machine is "due to hit" just because the number of hands defined as a cycle have been played on it without hitting a royal. Actually, the cycle is calculated as one divided by the probability of a royal flush on each play. In the long run, if you play a number of hands equal to n cycles you may "expect" n royal flushes, but the Poisson Distribution reveals your real probabilities.

Expected Value   The average payback of a particular play. Often abbreviated EV. See "What Does 'Expected Value' Really Mean?" on page 21 for more details.

Full Pay Usually the best payoff schedule offered for a particular game. There are exceptions, however, such as the enhanced full pay games. These include the 4700-coin royal or a bonus for a sequential royal at a few casinos and the 10/6 and 9/7 Jacks-or-Better games at the Stratosphere. Most strategies are developed initially for the full pay game, and sometimes they are modified for other variations.

Optimum Play Employing a strategy that may not be quite computer-perfect play but is designed to yield the maximum long term win rate with real human play. See "What Does 'Optimum Play' Really Mean?" on page 29 for more details.

Payback The long term expected return of a game as it is being played. Usually expressed as a percent. You can expect to make a profit on a game only if its payback (including any slot club rebate and/or comps) is over 100%. (See also "Rated Payback" below.)

Payoff The number of coins or credits paid for a particular winning hand, often expressed on a "per-coin" basis. For example, a Full House in standard full pay Jacks-or-Better with five coins bet pays 45 coins, but instead of 45-for-5 this is usually expressed as 9-for-1. Note the use of "for" rather than "to" for the payoff odds; this is because the bet has already disappeared into the guts of the machine, and a Full House returns nine coins or credits for each coin or credit bet, which is actually 8-to-1 odds.

Payout The actual dropping of coins by a machine. A hand pay is also considered to be a payout.

Penalty Card A discard that does not affect the chances of making the primary target hand but whose absence from the remaining deck reduces the chances of making some of the secondary payoffs, thus reducing the EV of the play. See "Secondary Payoff" below and "What Is A Penalty Card?" on page 28.

Perfect Play   Every play is made for the absolute highest expected value. Although perfect play is easy on a trivial game such as Double Down Stud, and not too difficult on Jacks-or-Better, it is nearly impossible for a human to achieve perfect play on the more complex games such as Double Bonus Poker.

Push   No exchange of money. A payoff equal to your bet is proclaimed by the machine to be a win, but actually the one-for-one payoff is a push. Compare this with a blackjack hand where you and the dealer each have eighteen (or any equivalent hands except when you bust).

Rated Payback   The long term expected return of a game assuming perfect play.

Secondary Payoff   In many cases we are drawing with the hopes of making a particular big payoff, but much of the expected value of the play comes from smaller payoffs when we miss the big one. For example, you might draw two cards to a royal flush but end up instead with a high pair, two pair, three-of-a-kind, a straight or a flush, all of which would be secondary payoffs.

Volatility Index   The standard deviation per unit bet. See "The Volatility Index" on page 23 in the text for more information.

Zilch   Nothing. In this book, the word "zilch" is used to designate a pre-draw hand with nothing worth holding (that is, you should redraw all five cards) or a final hand that does not yield a payoff.

Dan Paymar was born and raised in Flint, Michigan. Following four years at Michigan Tech, where he first started programming a computer in 1957, he spent a muggy summer in Cleveland, Ohio, maintaining several Bendix G-15 computers before transferring to Los Angeles to begin a career in logic design.

If you wonder why you've never heard of a Bendix computer, it's because the computer division was bought out by Control Data in 1963. This gave Dan the opportunity to become one of the first ever to have a "personal" computer—he bought a G-15 from the old stock that Control Data didn't want. This was a refrigerator-size monster that consumed about four kilowatts and was less powerful than today's $100 programmable pocket calculator; at the time, however, it represented a giant step up from the mechanical desk calculators.

Dan stayed with Control Data four more years then joined Encyclopædia Britannica in 1967 to develop a text editing system. Unfortunately, technology hadn't caught up with fantasy so the project never got off the ground. (Note that this was many years before laser printers and the desktop publishing revolution.)

Next, he joined two other engineers to start Educational Data Systems and shifted back to programming to write a BASIC language interpreter and disk operating system for the Data General Nova computer to handle up to sixteen users. As far as we know, this was the first time-sharing system to run on a minicomputer.

Educational Data Systems became Point 4 Data Corporation when the company began manufacturing its own computers. Meanwhile, Dan developed an accessory for the Apple-II computer, which he sold by mail and through retail stores. Realizing that the mail order business didn't have to tie him down, he and his family moved to Durango, Colorado, in 1980. In 1988 he returned to California to manage a computer repair store, but that business was mortally wounded by the government's "protective" import surtaxes on memory chips, so he chose to indulge in semiretirement, became a poker dealer and moved to Las Vegas.

That's where his interest in video poker began. His first endeavor was to survey the casinos and publish a directory of favorable video poker opportunities. Not satisfied with the strategies then available, he put his computer experience to use. He analyzed the games and published his results in the predecessor to this book, *Video Poker – Precision Play*. The book evolved and expanded, going through many revisions as new games began to appear and questions about how to play them arose. Now out of print, the tenth edition was the last version before this book.

Dan currently works part time as a poker dealer instructor and still plays video poker, but his primary interest is sharing his knowledge and information with others through his various publications. (See Appendix 5 for Dan's other products, or contact him online at *vptimes@lvcm.com.*

ConJelCo is a publisher based in Pittsburgh, Pennsylvania that specializes in books and software for the serious gambler. In addition to this book, ConJelCo publishes the book *Winning Low-Limit Hold'em* by Lee Jones, *Las Vegas Blackjack Diary* by Stuart Perry, *Hold'em Excellence* by Lou Krieger, *More Hold'em Excellence* by Lou Krieger, and several software products including *Blackjack Trainer* for the Macintosh and Windows, *Ken Elliott's CrapSim* for DOS, *Percentage Hold'em* for DOS, *Stud & Hold'em Poker* for Windows, the *Statistical Blackjack Analyzer* for Windows, and *StatKing* for Windows.

ConJelCo periodically publishes a newsletter, *The Intelligent Gambler*, sent free to our customers. *The Intelligent Gambler* carries articles by our authors as well as other respected authors in the gambling community. In addition, it is the source of information about new ConJelCo products and special offers.

ConJelCo also sells books, software and videos from other publishers. If you'd like a free catalog or to be put on the mailing list for *The Intelligent Gambler* you can write to us at:

> ConJelCo LLC
> 132 Radcliff Dr.
> Pittsburgh, PA 15237

Our phone number is 800-492-9210 (412-492-9210 outside of the U.S.), and our fax number is 412-492-9031.

ConJelCo is on the Internet. You can send electronic mail to us at *orders@conjelco.com*. From the World Wide Web you can reach us at URL *http://www.conjelco.com*. On our web server you'll find a complete, annotated, ConJelCo catalog, demos of software by ConJelCo and others, and lots of other goodies for the serious gambler.